THE SMART SET CONVERSATIONS

H. L. MENCKEN
GEORGE JEAN NATHAN

Introduction by Ether Editors

ETHER EDITIONS

The Smart Set Conversations [I-IX] originally appeared as individual columns in various issues of *The Smart Set* magazine during the years 1920-1923. The first of these conversations was authored by and appeared under the joint byline of H. L. Mencken and George Jean Nathan. The second through ninth conversations were also authored by H. L. Mencken and George Nathan but appeared under their joint pseudonym Major Owen Hatteras, D.S.O.

First Printing, 2023

THE SMART SET
CONVERSATIONS

CONTENTS

INTRODUCTION

On the eve of the First World War, two iconoclastic young journalists were offered the co-editorship of a magazine that was clearly in trouble at the time. The magazine was *The Smart Set*, a monthly with literary ambitions and editorial offices in New York. The young iconoclasts were H. L. Mencken and George Jean Nathan, two writers possessing no small ambition of their own but with little else in common save for their mutual contempt for mediocrity and pretentiousness, literary or otherwise. During their nine years as co-editors, from 1914 until 1923, Mencken and Nathan transformed *The Smart Set* into a must-read of the early jazz era, established themselves as two of America's foremost critics, and became bona fide celebrities in American popular culture. Indeed, "Mencken and Nathan" were at times as popular collectively as they were separately.

Among their many writings in *The Smart Set* are a jointly authored series of nine "Conversations," written dialogues between Mencken and Nathan that depict their personal interactions in various circumstances and locales, chronicling a series of events perhaps both real and imagined. The "Conversations" vary in length, running from a low of about 2,700+ words to a high of about 4,400+ words. Although Mencken and Nathan were certainly familiar with the structure of dramatic literature, especially as it appeared in the published plays of the era, they seldom employed the textual apparatus typical of playwriting in their "Conversations." Descriptions of action, business, and stage directions, for example, appear infrequently. Additional characters rarely appear and seem more an afterthought in closing. Taken together, these

"Conversations" offer a plausible if somewhat exaggerated representation of their idiosyncratic relationship as authors and editors. *The Smart Set* "Conversations" of H. L. Mencken and George Jean Nathan are reprinted in the present edition in their entirety.

Founded in 1900 by William D'Alton Mann, a veteran of the American Civil War, successful railroad man, and restless entrepreneur, *The Smart Set* was originally published with the stated intention of entertaining "smart people," at least as Mann would then define them.[1] The "Colonel," as he styled himself, had previously achieved some success with a weekly entitled *Town Topics*, a New York scandal sheet that has been likened to a "front for a blackmail operation."[2] *The Smart Set* was intended to provide less scandal and more literature, albeit for the same New York society readership that devoured *Town Topics*. During its first decade, *The Smart Set* offered a popular, though stubbornly low-paying venue for writers both established and unknown. Early contributors to the magazine included notable American fiction writers Ambrose Bierce, James Branch Cabell, Theodore Dreiser, O. Henry, and Jack London.[3]

H. L. Mencken, then a journalist of increasing stature with the Baltimore *Sun* and author of books on George Bernard Shaw and Frederick Nietzsche, joined *The Smart Set* as book critic in 1908. The always prolific Mencken continued to maintain his position with the *Sun* when he took on the task of writing a monthly column of literary criticism for *The Smart Set* that November. George Jean Nathan's career began at the New York *Herald*, where he was initially hired as a reporter. In addition to his work at the *Herald*, Nathan began writing for periodicals, including *The Bohemian* and *Harper's Weekly*, where he drew greater notice for his coverage of the theater scene. Nathan became *The Smart Set* drama critic in October the following year.[4]

Mencken was the slightly older of the two. Born in 1880 in Baltimore, Maryland to parents of German ancestry, he would remain a resident of the city throughout his life, and always took great pride in his German roots. First educated outside the home at the private Knapp's

Institute, his formal education was completed at the public Baltimore Polytechnic. Mencken was a voracious reader, and though a college education was certainly accessible for him, he chose not to pursue one. Instead, he went to work in the family cigar business and took writing courses via correspondence school, intending to launch a career in journalism. His father's early death relieved him of further responsibilities to the family business, and in 1899 he landed an entry-level job at the Baltimore *Morning Herald*, where his lengthy newspaper career began in earnest.[5]

Nathan was born in 1882 in Fort Wayne, Indiana to midwestern parents of European Jewish ancestry. Six years later the family moved to Cleveland, Ohio. His father was a successful wholesaler in wines and spirits and provided the young Nathan with a good education that included tutors at home in addition to his local schooling. Two of Nathan's uncles played significant roles in contributing to his early interest in the theater. One was a theatrical promoter, the other a critic for the New York *Herald* and other publications. By the time he left Cleveland, Nathan had already witnessed performances by some of the most celebrated players of the era. He went on to attend university at Cornell, where he enjoyed the life of a clubman and excelled at fencing. After Cornell, Nathan studied in Italy before eventually settling in New York, where he was hired as a reporter at the *Herald*. Ill-suited to a reporter's beat, Nathan chose instead to focus his writing on the entertainment world.[6]

If their later memories serve, Mencken and Nathan first met in New York in May 1908. Details of this meeting vary, but it likely occurred as they were each being considered for positions at *The Smart Set*. It is also likely that after their initial meeting, an unrecorded number of cocktails followed hard upon at the nearby Café des Beaux Arts.[7] Sitting together over drinks, the two men must have offered quite the visual contrast. According to a writer who knew them both, "Nathan was slight, dark-haired, dark-eyed, swarthy, and Semitic; Mencken was stocky, blonde, blue-eyed, and Nordic."[8] It is also likely that their contrasting taste in clothes was also in stark relief. Outward differences aside, Mencken and Nathan found common ground in both intellect and perspective. Both agreed there were icons to be dislodged from their pedestals and "imbecilities" to be exposed. Surveying the contemporary literary scene, the newly acquainted H. L. Mencken and George Jean Nathan considered themselves excellent candidates for the task at hand, and they agreed that *The Smart Set* could serve as a useful springboard for their performance of such work.

During their early years as contributors to *The Smart Set*, Mencken and Nathan produced an editorially diverse collection of writings for the magazine. Shortest among them were hundreds of anonymous epigrams, brief witticisms which a clever promoter would occasionally repackage as preview fodder for silent movie screens.[9] Mencken and Nathan have rightly been called masters of the epigram as a literary form, and they would often solicit such *bon mots* from other writers for anonymous inclusion in *The Smart Set*.[10]

Throughout their tenure as both contributors and editors, Mencken and Nathan experimented with different writing styles in various columns and incidental pieces, some written individually, some jointly, some signed under their own names and others printed under pseudonyms. The most memorable pseudonym to appear in *The Smart Set* was that of Owen Hatteras, shared at various times by Mencken, Nathan, and several other contributors. Owen Hatteras first appeared in the April 1912 issue as the pseudonymous author of a new column entitled "Pertinent and Impertinent." Mencken, always the more prolific writer, would appear under the Owen Hatteras byline and numerous other pseudonyms throughout his tenure at *The Smart Set*.

During their co-editorship of the magazine, Mencken and Nathan would go on to produce other columns together, such as "Répétition Générale," signed under their owns names, as well as a series of "Conversations" on various topics, always written by the two of them but most often signed under their frequently used joint pseudonym, Owen Hatteras. Of course, the most polished and substantial writings that

Mencken and Nathan contributed to *The Smart Set* were their signed monthly columns of literary and dramatic criticism. These columns always appeared at the end of the magazine, where more discerning readers would usually begin each issue.[11] Here, in so many choice words, Mencken could help make or break an author's literary career, while Nathan could contribute to the success or failure of a Broadway production.

Once they were firmly established as regular columnists, Mencken and Nathan would both survive the revolving door then typical among editorial staff in magazine publishing, as well as the inevitable changes in corporate ownership of *The Smart Set*. Such changes were usually precipitated by fluctuations in circulation and, consequently, in advertising revenues.

Eventually tiring of the magazine, due in part to self-inflicted legal wounds resulting from his tactics at *Town Topics*, William D'Alton Mann sold *The Smart Set* to John Adams Thayer in 1911. Thayer had previously excelled in the advertising side of the publishing business and hoped to achieve similar success as the new owner of *The Smart Set*. But after three difficult years, including the tumultuous one-year editorship of Willard Huntington Wright, whose influence on the magazine remains underappreciated, Thayer sold *The Smart Set* to Eugene F. Crowe, one of his creditors, and Eltinge F. Warner, the successful publisher of outdoor magazine *Field and Stream*. By then, it had become clear to loyal readers of *The Smart Set* that Mencken and Nathan *were* the magazine, a notion that would dawn upon its new owners soon enough.

The events that led H. L. Mencken and George Jean Nathan to become co-editors of *The Smart Set* have been retold on numerous occasions in what might be called "the overcoat anecdote." In gist, Eltinge F. Warner, soon to be responsible for making *The Smart Set* a profitable enterprise, was returning from abroad on the eve of the First World War aboard the *Imperator*, then a cruise ship of the Hamburg America Line. Out on deck for a brisk stroll, he happened upon a man wearing an overcoat similar or perhaps identical to his own. The two men compared notes on their "exclusive" London tailor and subsequently shared conversation over drinks. The other man aboard the *Imperator* was George Jean Nathan, drama critic for *The Smart Set*. When it later came time for Warner to appoint a new editor at the magazine, he remembered Nathan from their shipboard happenstance and asked him if he would be interested in the position. Nathan agreed on the condition that H. L. Mencken would join him in a similar capacity.[12]

Mencken would later recall that he and Nathan had both been offered the editorship of *The Smart Set* toward the end of the Thayer regime. "Every time I saw him [Thayer]," Mencken wrote, "he besought me to take the editorship, and when I declined, he offered it to Nathan, but both of us, by this time, had become so firmly convinced that he was an incurable jackass that we wanted to have no truck with him."[13] But on this occasion, under new ownership, a bargain was struck. It was a financially attractive arrangement which included partial ownership incentives in the magazine for Mencken and Nathan as co-editors. Warner wisely assumed responsibility for business affairs, and with equal wisdom left the two young iconoclasts in complete editorial control of *The Smart Set*.

Both men must have known what they were getting into, having spent the previous six years as regular columnists for the magazine and watching more than one editor come and go. In business terms, the financial health of *The Smart Set*, with its heavy debt burden and roller-coaster circulation figures, was a poorly kept secret. Drastic measures had to be taken for the magazine to survive, much less flourish. Under the new ownership of Crowe and Warner, most of the staff were let go and the magazine's offices were relocated to more affordable quarters.[14] In terms of editorial content, the task of turning *The Smart Set* around would fall squarely on the shoulders of H. L. Mencken and George Jean Nathan, who would take drastic measures of their own to keep the magazine in print.

Once in harness, Mencken and Nathan divided their editorial responsibilities in a practical if uncommon manner. Essentially, Nathan ran the office in New York while Mencken remained in Baltimore, working his way through whatever came over the transom in search of publishable manuscripts. Mencken would later describe their editorial process as follows:

> Our authority as editors is exactly equal; nevertheless, we are never in conflict. I read all the manuscripts that are sent to us, and send Nathan those I think are fit to print. If he agrees, they go into type at once; if he dissents, they are rejected forthwith. This veto is absolute, and works both ways.... We employ no readers, and take no advice. Every piece of manuscript that comes into the office passes through my hands, or those of Nathan, and usually through the hands of both of us. I live in Baltimore, but come to New York every other week.[15]

Although payments to contributors would remain notoriously low, Nathan insisted that authors be paid promptly upon manuscript acceptance, rather than upon publication date. As Mencken recalled, "it was Nathan's belief, born of his wide experience with magazines, that most authors would make no protest against meagre pay if they got their money without delay....".[16]

With the September issue already on the street and the October issue in galley proofs, the November 1914 issue of *The Smart Set* was the first to be published with Mencken and Nathan in complete editorial control.[17] Their signed columns appeared at the end of the magazine, as usual. Nathan, writing in "The Trail of the Lonesome Spine," performed critical surgery upon several theatrical productions. In particular, he took a scalpel to Roi Cooper Megrue's otherwise financially successful play *Under Cover*, referring to it a "vertebræ-shivering sdrucciolamento," which was "from first to last perfectly artificial." Mencken followed with "Critics of More or Less Badness," in which he passed judgement, more or less, upon Lord Alfred Douglas' *Oscar Wilde and Myself* as being an "amazingly impudent and unpleasantly amusing book." Mencken subsequently digressed upon a few other works of non-fiction before finally confessing that he had altogether forgotten to offer his commentary on any works of fiction. The oversight would be rectified in subsequent issues.

In addition to their signed columns in the November issue, Nathan offered a story entitled "D.S.W." his acronym for "Doctor of the Science of Wooing." Mencken offered a novelette entitled "The Barbarous Bradley," in which the titular character attempts to sabotage his former lover's honeymoon. The pseudonymous Owen Hatteras returned with his critical observations on the great city of Philadelphia in "The City of Seven Sundays." Other contributors were familiar, some relatively new. They included a writer of mysterious origins named Achmed Abdullah, Canadian poet Bliss Carmen, New York author and playwright Percival Wilde, Arkansas-born storyteller Thyra Samter Winslow, and hailing from Maine, the recent Vassar graduate and promising young poet Edna St. Vincent Millay. But many contributors to the November issue of *The Smart Set* were complete unknowns. Among them, Raoul Della Torre (Mencken) offered a curious dialog entitled "Ah, Che La Morte!" R. B. McLoughlin (Mencken again) made a rare appearance with "The Rewards of Science," and William Fink (more Mencken) offered his "Thoughts on Mortality." Also making a rare appearance was Ronald V. Cross (Nathan) with a brief medical satire entitled "The Return of Baron Munchausen."

The following month, in the December 1914 issue, *The Smart Set* masthead finally reflected the changes that had recently taken place at the magazine. Below the title the credits read "Edited by George Jean Nathan and H. L. Mencken." Below the table of contents, the new editors promised an additional "Half a Hundred Burlesques, Epigrams, Poems, Short Satires, Etc." With these announcements, H. L. Mencken and George Jean Nathan, long the backbone of the magazine, were off and running on their new literary adventure as writers and editors.

Mencken always made good on his commitment to come north to assist Nathan in finalizing upcoming issues of *The Smart Set*. After taking the train from Baltimore to New York, he would usually stay at the Algonquin Hotel near Nathan's apartment in the Royalton. In Nathan's quarters, they would take up the magazine's editorial matters in more comfortable and private surroundings, both preferring to avoid any unnecessary appearance in the offices of *The Smart Set*.[18] As their co-editorship progressed, their social interactions with the many writers and editors among their acquaintance helped make manifest a curious joint persona, something they both willfully encouraged. Outside the pages of *The Smart Set*, "Mencken and Nathan" were often seen and heard together at the tables of the popular dining and drinking establishments they frequented. Conspicuous at any literary or social event, they were always sought-after conversationalists among guests at the more intimate gatherings they attended.

The editorial practices of Messrs. Mencken and Nathan, as exhibited in the first issue of *The Smart Set* they could rightly claim as their own, were really nothing new. Certainly not to them. Rather, they were practices borne of necessity, honed from six years of previous experience during their early tenure as contributors to the magazine. During their nine years as co-editors, from 1914 through 1923, George Jean Nathan and H. L. Mencken brought out a new issue of *The Smart Set* every month, a task they usually performed with *elan*.

The United States had not yet entered the First World War in 1914, but nevertheless, domestic tensions regarding the conflict rose exponentially during the next few years. While they were hardly immune to the war and its impact on their personal and professional lives, Mencken and Nathan made the joint decision to keep *The Smart Set* out of the conflict from an editorial standpoint. This was especially prudent where Mencken was concerned, given his often-enunciated predilections toward all things German. Instead, they focused on what Mencken later cited as their "proper business, which was the printing of the best stuff in prose or verse that we could find."[19]

During the latter half of the decade, while maintaining their roles as co-editors of *The Smart Set*, Mencken and Nathan both contributed to other publications and authored several books, most separately, some jointly. After a few less-than-successful experiences with other publishers, including Mencken's friend and correspondent Philip Goodman, arguably a better Broadway producer than book publisher, Mencken and Nathan would henceforth bring their book-length works to the attention of Alfred A. Knopf, whose up-and-coming firm would publish works by both men throughout the remainder of their careers.

A few of the books Mencken and Nathan produced during this period were rather slight. Others were more substantial. In 1916, Mencken authored *A Book of Burlesques* and *A Little Book in C Major*. Both were short works and included some writings harvested from *The Smart Set*. Among his more distinctive efforts were *A Book of Prefaces* (1917), which considered the authors Joseph Conrad, Theodore Dreiser, and James Gibbons Huneker, as well as the subject of Puritanism in American literature; a unique philological work entitled *The American Language* (1919); and the first book in what became a multi-volume series entitled *Prejudices* (1919). In the first volumes of his *Prejudices* series, Mencken often reworked material from some of his previously published writings from *The Smart Set*. During this same period, Nathan authored short works including *Bottoms Up: An Application of the Slapstick to Satire* (1917) and *A Book Without a Title* (1918). His better-realized works, all focused on the world in which he was most comfortable as author and critic, included *Another Book on the Theatre* (1915), *Mr. George Jean Nathan Presents* (1917), and *The Popular Theatre* (1918). Nathan possessed equally fertile resources to draw upon from his previous writings in *The Smart Set*.

Also published during this period was their jointly authored work, *The American Credo: A Contribution Toward the Interpretation of the National Mind* (1920). *The American Credo* was a humorous and often scathing assessment of what some Americans of the period appeared to believe to be true, expressed in short phrases such as these:

#8: That the lions in the cage which a lion-tamer enters are always sixty years old and have had all their teeth pulled.

#34: That one can never tell accurately what the public wants.

#101: That German babies are brought up on beer in place of milk.

#238: That a man is always a much heartier eater than a woman.

#376: That an old woman with rheumatism in her leg can infallibly predict when it is going to rain.

#444: That whenever there is a rough-house during a strike, it is caused by foreign anarchists who are trying to knock out American idealism.[20]

Mencken once told his early bibliographer Carroll Frey that "*The American Credo* was Nathan's idea, not mine; I did only the preface." However, Mencken would later recall having written many of the credos himself. Whatever the case with respect to individual authorship of the credos, Mencken and Nathan shared the proceeds of the book "fifty-fifty."[21]

Mencken and Nathan also collaborated on a full-length play entitled *Heliogabalus: A Buffoonery in Three Acts* (1920). *Heliogabalus* was published by Alfred A. Knopf and appeared under their own names. Although most of the writing credit for this work should be attributed to the more prolific Mencken, Nathan's theatrical perspective was no doubt invaluable in developing the structure of the work. Very loosely based on the youthful Elagabalus (circa 204-222), briefly the Emperor of Rome (circa 218-222), Mencken described the origins of the play to bibliographer Frey as follows:

One afternoon Nathan and I were sitting in his apartment at the Royalton, in Forty-Fourth Street, New York, and fell into a discussion of playwriting. We came to the conclusion that writing a play was a much smaller job than writing a book, and decided to write one to prove it. I contended that a so-called plot was unnecessary; that all that was needed was an amusing character. "Very well," said Nathan, "but where is your character?" I had just been re-reading Edgar Saltus' *Imperial Purple*, and Heliogabalus came to mind. We then went to Rogers', in Sixth Avenue, for dinner. By the time we got it down *Heliogabalus* was planned, and six weeks later it was finished. I still believe somehow that, as plays go, it is not a bad one. Writing it turned out to be absurdly easy — in fact, a sort of holiday from criticism. I ceased to respect dramatists from that time. Their work, I am convinced, is child's play.[22]

Surely their most curious literary collaboration of the period was the satirical dual biography *Pistols for Two*. The title of the work, of course, suggests a sort of literary *duel* between its two biographical subjects, H. L. Mencken and George Jean Nathan. Published by Knopf in 1917 and running scarcely over 12,000 words, *Pistols for Two* was jointly written by Mencken and Nathan but appeared under their frequently used pseudonym Owen Hatteras. This brief work contains a series of occasionally believable and by turns self-aggrandizing and self-mocking biographical observations on the two men, both in terms of their individual lives and in their roles as co-editors of *The Smart Set*. The first lines in their individual biographies are illustrative of the work:

George Jean Nathan

He was born in Fort Wayne, Indiana, February 14 and 15 (the stunning event occurred precisely at 12 midnight) 1882.

His boyhood ambition was to be an African explorer in a pith helmet, with plenty of room on the chest ribbon for medals that would be bestowed upon him by the beauteous Crown Princess of Luxembourg.

He was educated at Cornell University and the University of Bologna, in Italy.

He is a man of middle height, straight, slim, dark, with eyes like the middle of August, black hair which he brushes back *à la française*, and a rather sullen mouth.

He smokes from the moment his man turns off the matutinal showerbath until his man turns it on again at bedtime.

He rarely eats meat.

He lives in a bachelor apartment, nearly one-third of which is occupied by an ice-box containing refreshing beverages. On the walls of his apartment are the pictures of numerous toothsome creatures. He is at the present time occupied in writing a book describing his sentimental adventures among them.[23]

H. L. Mencken

He was born at Baltimore on Sunday, September 12, 1880, and was baptized in the Church of England.

He was educated at the Baltimore Polytechnic, and is theoretically competent to run a steam engine or a dynamo, but actually is quite incapable of doing either.

Down to the age of fifteen it was his ambition to be a chemist, and to this day he is full of fantastic chemical information and fond of unloading it. At the age of fourteen he invented a means of toning photographic silver prints with platinum.

The family business was tobacco, and he was drafted for it on leaving school. He became a journeyman cigar-maker, and can make excellent cigars to this day. But when chemistry and business died out, literature set in, and he took to journalism.

At the age of twenty-three he was city editor and at twenty-five managing editor of the Baltimore *Herald*, now defunct —

the youngest managing editor of a big city daily in the United States.

He printed a book of poems at twenty-two — now a rare *bibelot*. He was "discovered," as the saying is, by Ellery Sedgwick, now editor of the *Atlantic Monthly*, but then running *Leslie's Monthly*. He and Sedgwick have remained on friendly terms to this day, but he sometimes writes for the *Atlantic*.[24]

Pistols for Two presents an interesting case in determining who wrote what in certain literary collaborations between Mencken and Nathan. Regarding the origins of this joint title, bibliographer Carroll Frey stated that "Mencken wrote the sketch of Nathan and the introductory and closing remarks. Nathan wrote the sketch of Mencken."[25] In the introduction to his bibliography, Frey also acknowledged his reliance upon Mencken himself for details about the various works considered therein.

Mencken and Nathan were both great spoofers. Mencken's talent for the literary prank is perhaps best revealed in his infamous "bathtub hoax," a fictitious history of the bathtub perpetrated upon the reading public in an article entitled "A Neglected Anniversary" which appeared in the *New York Evening Mail* during the same year as *Pistols for Two*. While it is certainly conceivable that Mencken and Nathan wrote the biographical sketches of each other in *Pistols for Two*, and it is true that most bibliographers and biographers have repeated Frey's assertions that each wrote the biography of the other, both men would later suggest that quite the opposite was the case. In a letter to the editor appearing in the *New York Times*, published as a follow-up to his review of *Disturber of the Peace*, William Manchester's biography of Mencken, George Jean Nathan wrote that "the reference to Mencken in 'Pistols for Two' was written not by Nathan but by Mencken himself and attributed facetiously to Nathan."[26] Discussing *Pistols for Two* in his memoir *My Life as Author and Editor*, Mencken stated that he "wrote all of it save Nathan's biography of himself."[27] The style and substance of their separate biographical texts, as they appear in *Pistols for Two*, offer further proof of authorship.

Apart from their own endeavors and their many contributions to *The Smart Set*, Mencken and Nathan frequently nurtured new talent in the pages of the magazine. Conspicuous among them were F. Scott Fitzgerald, later author of *The Great Gatsby*, whose early stories including "Babes in the Woods" and "The Diamond as Big as the Ritz" arguably helped launch his career as a novelist. The versatile storyteller Thyra Samter Winslow, whose stories were a favorite of both Mencken and Nathan, appeared in numerous issues. She was perhaps the most prolific contributor to the magazine besides Mencken and Nathan themselves. The future Hollywood screenwriter Ben Hecht, then writing for the Chicago *Daily News*, made frequent appearances in *The Smart Set*. Another newcomer who eventually found his way into the magazine was Dashiell Hammett, who would later achieve fame with his Sam Spade novel *The Maltese Falcon*.

In his youth, Mencken had published a book of poetry entitled *Ventures into Verse*, but neither he nor Nathan ever claimed to be astute judges of the literary form. Nevertheless, they published the likes of Robinson Jeffers, Luis Muñoz Marín, John McClure, Ezra Pound, Pulitzer Prize winner Sara Teasdale, George Sterling, Louis Untermeyer, and other poets in the pages of *The Smart Set*. Dramatic works were also well-represented in the magazine with occasional contributions by the all-around man of the theater George M. Cohan, a few short compositions by the long-time Mencken correspondent Theodore Dreiser, and an early appearance by a promising new playwright named Eugene O'Neill, whose play *The Long Voyage Home* appeared in the October 1917 issue of the magazine.[28]

Although the appearance of writings by foreign authors had substantially diminished after Willard Huntington Wright's short-lived tenure as editor and continued to wane during the war years, Mencken and Nathan published several notable authors then writing from abroad. Among them were the Russian novelist and playwright Leonid

Andreyev, French dramatist Eugène Brieux, English novelists Aleister Crowley and Hugh Walpole, and Anglo-Irish writer Lord Dunsany. Two stories from *Dubliners* by the Irish author James Joyce made an early appearance in *The Smart Set*.

During their tenure as co-editors at *The Smart Set*, "Mencken and Nathan" earned a substantial degree of dual notoriety, and collective sobriquets were often bestowed upon them in the popular press. Writing in The Brooklyn *Daily Eagle*, the poet John A. V. Weaver, himself an occasional contributor to *The Smart Set*, once referred to Mencken and Nathan as "The T.N.T. Twins."[29] Another writer cited theirs as among "Ten Historic Partnerships." To wit:

1. Damon and Pythias
2. Lea and Perrin
3. Fast and Furious
4. Scotch and Soda
5. Bright and Early
6. Black and White
7. Bread and Cheese
8. Half and Half
9. Gin and Gingerale
10. Mencken and Nathan[30]

Perhaps the most memorable contemporary observation on the literary partnership between H. L. Mencken and George Jean Nathan was conveyed in a parody written in the style of Eugene Field's "Wynken, Blynken, and Nod" by the poet Berton Braley. Entitled "Three — Minus One," it originally appeared in the New York *Sun* on December 3rd, 1920.

> There were three that sailed away one night
> Far from the maddening throng;

And two of the three were always right
    And every one else was wrong.
But they took another along, these two;
    To bear them company,
For He was the only One ever knew
    Why the other two should Be;
    And so they sailed away, these three —
        Mencken,
        Nathan
        And God.

And the two they talked of the aims of art,
    Which they alone understood;
And they quite agreed from the very start
    That nothing was any good
Except some novels that Dreiser wrote
    And some plays from Germany.
When God objected — they rocked the boat
    And dropped him into the sea,
    "For you have no critical facultee,"
        Said Mencken
        And Nathan
        To God.

The two came cheerfully sailing home
    Over the surging tide
And trod once more on their native loam
    Wholly self-satisfied;
And the little group that calls them great
    Welcomed them fawningly,
Though why the rest of us tolerate
    This precious pair must be
    Something nobody else can see,

> But Mencken,
> Nathan
> And God![31]

Mencken and Nathan were both profiled by journalist Isaac Goldberg during the mid-1920s. Goldberg, a versatile writer for the Boston *Evening Transcript*, initially published short sketches of *The Smart Set* co-editors for the Haldeman-Julius Company's *Little Blue Book* series. These two sketches (Mencken was #611; Nathan was #843) were the impetus for Goldberg's full-length biographical works subsequently published by Simon and Schuster in 1925 (Mencken) and 1926 (Nathan).

Much later in life, Mencken and Nathan both experienced the sort of celebrity comeuppance that often results from a long and active career in the public arena. George Jean Nathan got his due as the fictional drama critic Addison DeWitt in the classic film *All About Eve* (1950). For his portrayal of DeWitt, the classic Hollywood heavy George Sanders won the Academy Award for Best Supporting Actor. *All About Eve* was directed by Joseph L. Mankiewicz and based on an original story by Mary Orr. Several years later, in the Broadway play *Inherit the Wind* (1955), H. L. Mencken was portrayed by a young Tony Randall in the character of fictional newspaper reporter E. K. Hornbeck. Like Mencken, the opinionated young Hornbeck covered the controversy over teaching evolution in the 1925 Scopes Monkey Trial. Originally written for the stage by Jerome Lawrence and Robert E. Lee, a later film version (1960) directed by Stanley Kramer would find Gene Kelly cast in the role of Hornbeck.

When H. L. Mencken and George Jean Nathan wrote separately in *The Smart Set*, Mencken was, as previously stated, the more prolific of the two, certainly in terms of mere word count but also in the number of his pseudonymous appearances in the magazine. When writing jointly, the length of Mencken's contributions to an individual column or incidental piece would usually surpass that of Nathan, again in terms of word count, and often by half. Nevertheless, whenever they wrote together, under their own names or under a pseudonym, their work in *The Smart Set* took on a unique literary voice all its own.

Among their joint contributions to *The Smart Set* are the nine "Conversations" reprinted herein. These dialogues between H. L. Mencken and George Jean Nathan appeared during the last few years of their editorial partnership at the magazine, a period during which their personal and professional relationships were arguably at their zenith. At different instances, these "Conversations" consist of biographical revelations, exercises in mutual entertainment, literary one upmanship, stand-up comedy, ironic and satirical social commentary, and occasional self-promotion. Throughout, they present "Mencken and Nathan" to their readership as perhaps they wished to be imagined and remembered. Clearly, these two men knew each other and their mutual foibles all too well. When writing together, they could be depended upon to hold court with ease on topics of varying consequence, all the while without taking themselves too seriously.

In April 1919 Mencken and Nathan launched a new column in *The Smart Set* entitled "Répétition Générale," signed under the joint byline George Jean Nathan and H. L. Mencken. While "Répétition Générale" would always be credited to them both, the ordering of their names would switch back and forth during the entire run of the column, which continued for the remainder of their co-editorship of the magazine. Their first "Conversation," entitled "On Theater-Going," appeared in the August 1920 issue of *The Smart Set* as the introductory portion of their regular "Répétition Générale" column. This first "Conversation," perhaps conceived as another of their many editorial experiments, was a departure in style and substance from previous appearances of "Répétition Générale," which had been devoted to observations on a broad range of issues and written in prose rather than as dialog. After the initial appearance of their first "Conversation," the "Répétition Générale" column would revert to its previous format, and the subsequent "Conversations" between Mencken and Nathan would appear as a stand-alone column under the telling byline, "Set Down by Major Owen Hatteras."

The Owen Hatteras byline and its various iterations in *The Smart Set* (Owen Hatteras, Major Owen Hatteras, Major Owen Hatteras, D.S.O.) had long since become the magazine's "'house pseudonym,' occasionally being signed to the second or third pieces in an issue by some regular contributor, often to the writer's amazement."[32] Owen Hatteras was indeed possessed of an impressive lineage. Though primarily the work of H. L. Mencken and secondarily, as in the case of their "Conversations," the work of Mencken and Nathan writing together, the pseudonym has also been ascribed to works by the former editor of *The Smart Set*, Willard Huntington Wright, poet John McClure, artist and writer Charles G. Shaw, and storyteller Thyra Samter Winslow.[33] Other writers likely appeared under the Owen Hatteras byline but have yet to be authoritatively identified.

The appearance of Conversation I: "On Theater-Going" in their August 1920 column "Répétition Générale" resulted in the establishment of a new column entitled "Conversations," subsequently numbered II-IX, and further delineated by topical sub-titles, such as "On Women," "On Politics" and "On Literature." Authorship for "Conversations" II-IX was thereafter attributed to Owen Hatteras, in one iteration or another, but typically with an acknowledgement of his military rank (Major) and his decoration, D.S.O. (Distinguished Service Order), both bestowed upon his fictitious character by virtue of his equally fictitious service during the First World War.

Attributing their subsequent "Conversations" to Owen Hatteras, surely the most venerable of *The Smart Set* pseudonyms, enabled Mencken and Nathan to indulge in certain literary, personal, political, and social discussions that were merely attributed to them, thereby establishing the pretense that their words were recorded at one remove, second-hand, by a third party. Hence the byline reading "Set Down" by the ubiquitous Owen Hatteras. This literary device must have worked to their satisfaction, and no doubt provided contemporary readers of

The Smart Set with an insider's glimpse of the familiar guise by which the authorial voices of H. L. Mencken and George Jean Nathan could be newly appreciated.

Conversations II: "On Anatomy and Physiology," as "Set Down by Major Owen Hatteras," established the uniformity of style by which the subsequent "Conversations" would appear. The topic for discussion, while not necessarily adhered to consistently throughout, is identified in subtitle, time and place are established, and the conversation ensues.

While certain locales indicated in the "Conversations" are easy enough to envisage, such as the dining room of the Ritz or the steps of St. Patrick's Cathedral, some situations as presented simply strain credulity. The morning scene at Muldoon's Health Farm in Conversation VIII: "On Marriage," is a case in point. Readers may find it hard to believe that Mencken and Nathan would attend a spa together, especially given the rigorous expectations of the celebrated former professional wrestler and proprietor William Muldoon. And for two men of vigorous smoking and drinking habits, the latter perhaps frustrated but seldom impeded during their experiences under Prohibition, a venue such as Campbell's Funeral Church from Conversation VII: "On Editing a Magazine" seems much more plausible.

Conversation IX: "On the Darker Races," appeared in the March 1923 issue of *The Smart Set*. It was the last "Conversation" between H. L. Mencken and George Jean Nathan, as "Set Down by Major Owen Hatteras, D.S.O.," to appear in the magazine. A close reading of this "Conversation" suggests that beneath their gratuitous use of colloquialisms and racial slurs, Mencken and Nathan intended to draw attention to what was then the highly controversial topic of "miscegenation." At the time this "Conversation" was published, there were still laws on the books against inter-racial marriage in dozens of states in the United States. It is surely no coincidence that the subtitle of this "Conversation" is shared with another influential publication of the era, *The Crisis: Record of the Darker Races*, published by the National Association for the Advancement of Colored People. *The Crisis* was then edited by W. E. B. Du Bois, whose compelling essay "The Superior Race" appeared in *The Smart Set* the following month.

Mencken and Nathan were controversial figures in their era, especially during their editorship of *The Smart Set*. They were two of the most prolific culture warriors of the early 1920s; disruptors, instigators, offensive to many, often by intent. Both men approached their roles as authors and critics with fearlessness and zeal. During their tenure at *The Smart Set*, they were vocal champions of free speech in the arts, in literature and in society. They were contemptuous of any attempts by government or institutions to censor the voice of the individual. In the same instance, the text and tone of their "Conversations" will serve to remind modern readers of certain blatant individual and societal prejudices that were casually and widely expressed in the United States during the early 20th century.

H. L. Mencken and his writings have been thoroughly considered by numerous biographers with respect to his expressions of antisemitism, misogyny, and racism. George Jean Nathan has, for the most part, escaped similar scrutiny, save for suggestions that he preferred to avoid discussion of his Jewish heritage.[34] Nathan's life, however, has yet to be fully realized by an authoritative biographer. Mencken has suffered from occasional cultural appropriation in the modern era and remains a polarizing figure.[35] Nathan has all but receded into obscurity. When considered together, Mencken and Nathan are clearly two men "of their times," and whether writing in an ironic and satirical voice or expressing firmly held personal beliefs, their "Conversations" offer a timely reflection on the history of the American public dialog.

Mencken and Nathan may have occasionally put words in each other's mouths in their "Conversations," if for no other reason than to help each other stay on topic or to simply move the dialog along. However, no definitive evidence of such a practice is known. But there is some indication that Mencken and Nathan may have considered using the "Conversations" as the basis for a new book about their professional lives as co-editors of *The Smart Set*. In his early biography of

Mencken, Isaac Goldberg refers to a series of letters between Mencken and Nathan that may have been intended to form the basis of a joint work, possibly to be entitled *Two Editors*.[36] Although Goldberg's reference to such an endeavor is otherwise vague and unsubstantiated, an example of Mencken's correspondence with the San Francisco poet and *Smart Set* contributor George Sterling serves to support the premise for such a work.

In Conversation IV: "On Politics," Nathan teases Mencken about the latter's arduous experience in covering the 1920 Democratic National Convention:

> "In order to enjoy the show you describe, you had to submit to innumerable intolerable inconveniences. You had to read the New York *Times* every day for two or three years. You had to wade through Woodrow's proclamations to the boobery. You had to flay your reason with the *Congressional Record*. And in the end you had to go to Chicago and half sweat to death, and then go to San Francisco and let George Sterling poison you with wood alcohol. All the while, I was quietly roosting here in New York, devoting myself to literature, tasty booze, and the chatter of amusing wenches."

George Sterling, whose published correspondence with H. L. Mencken is both entertaining and revealing, read George Jean Nathan's foregoing dialog in *The Smart Set*, and wrote to Mencken with tongue in cheek, "I've seen your libel (of course you write *all* of 'Conversations') as to my wasting wood-alcohol on you, and have had several interviews with my attorney." In response, Mencken confided to Sterling, "We stopped the Conversations for fear that they were getting tiresome. I want to do two more — one on religion and the other on patriotism. If the book ever comes out there will also be one on women."[37]

Alas, no such book was forthcoming, and by the end of 1923, Mencken and Nathan had both outgrown the inevitable confines of

The Smart Set. Mencken, perhaps, more so than Nathan. In January 1924, they would go on to establish and co-edit a new magazine called the *American Mercury*, published by Alfred A. Knopf. While they would attempt to carry on their editorial partnership as it existed during *The Smart Set* years, their personal and professional relationships would soon change, and both men would begin to chart separate courses. After losing its star contributors and editors, and with the Great Depression looming on the horizon, *The Smart Set* would eventually cease publication in 1930. By that time, the celebrated editorial partnership of "Mencken and Nathan" was over.

It is unfortunate that a work such as *Two Editors*, either jointly authored by H. L. Mencken and George Jean Nathan or pseudonymously attributed to Owen Hatteras, has never appeared. However, we do have their "Conversations." At various turns lowly colloquial, highly literate, ironic and satirical, rambling and contemplative, often hilarious, arguably troubling in text and tone, *The Smart Set* "Conversations" remain a curious and revealing record of the relationship between two of the twentieth century's most iconoclastic authors and editors, H. L. Mencken and George Jean Nathan.

———————————

A Note on the Text

The following nine "Conversations," written by H. L. Mencken and George Jean Nathan and appearing under their joint byline or under the pseudonymous byline of Owen Hatteras, have been fully transcribed from their original appearances in *The Smart Set*. In the present edition of the "Conversations," some of the original header information in the individual columns has been slightly modified in terms of capitalization, style, and punctuation, for the sake of textual uniformity. The individual appearances of the "Conversations" and their issue dates are fully delineated under Sources.

Conversation I: "On Theater-Going"

Scene: *The Fifth Avenue dining room in Delmonico's.*
Time: *Dinner is just done.*

Nathan

I thought you might like to put in the evening at the theater. I have two tickets for . . .

Mencken

Thanks excessively, but you may give your second ticket to the waiter, or shove it down the neck of that fat girl over yonder. I have a last come to a firm resolution: I shall never enter a theater again in this life.

Nathan

Well, old cock, you miss a lot.

Mencken

Exactly. I miss a lot of balderdash. I miss such puerilities as would make even a Congressman or a university president turn sick. For four or five years past you have been luring me into the theater now and then — and every time, without a single exception, I have been full of malaise for two days afterward. Do you remember that you took me to the first night of "Common Clay"? And to "Remnant," the night John Williams fell over the cuspidor? And to "Curiosity," down in Greenwich Village? And to Tom Dixon's anti-Bolshevist play, with the hooch dance? And to "Tiger! Tiger!"? And to "Up in Mabel's Room"? And to see Robert Mantell?

Nathan

You have run in bad luck.

Mencken

Precisely. If I live to be a thousand years old I'll never forget that performance of "Common Clay," with John Mason moaning and snorting around the stage like a saloon keeper raided by the police, and poor old Paul Armstrong out on the sidewalk arguing that it was a masterpiece spoiled by some obscure stage-manager. I drank more that night than is good for a man of my learning. I swore by the Lord God that I'd never enter an American theater again. But I went back — not once, but a dozen times. Now I propose to keep my oath at last. Honour is honour.

Nathan

You speak, characteristically, like a nanny-goat. Because you have seen a dozen or two bad plays, you forget that now and then there is a good one. You simply don't know the theater.

Mencken

With the highest respect, Bah! I was in active practice as a dramatic critic for six or seven years. I was the first critic in Christendom ever to write a book on Shaw. I am the only American who has ever edited Ibsen. I am familiar with the drama of eight or ten countries, including the Scandinavian. I constantly read plays, both printed and in manuscript, and have a very good collection of dramatic literature, including the largest Ibsen collection in the world.

Nathan

Piquant, and highly interesting! Yet all your lofty boasting simply bears out my case. I didn't say that you weren't familiar with the drama; I said that you weren't familiar with the theater. The two are quite distinct. You read too many plays, and don't see enough. What you overlook is that the performance of a play is not merely the intoning of the lines by a herd of pantaloons. It is, above all, a show. It is ocular. One goes to a bad play, but sees a pretty wench. It is enough. One goes to a worse play, and sees two pretty wenches. It is more than enough.

Mencken

Don't go any further. Even one is more than enough. I can't imagine getting any pleasure out of sitting in a stuffy theater, and gaping at a sweet baggage in company with a thousand shoe-drummers, song-writers, actors out of work, Grand Archons of the Knights of Pythias, curb-brokers, press-agents, loose women, clergymen off on toots, persons who believe in Jacksonian democracy, newspaper reporters and unhappy wives. Granted that a genuinely cute one comes out to show herself off. What is the fun staring at her from a distance, with the footlights between and a couple of police sergeants lolling about in the rear? When I happen upon a pretty gal who entertains my eye I like to engage her in conversation, and perhaps chuck her under the chin. What a pleasure it is to observe her manœuvres in the presence of a literary gent — her swift launching into the subject of Rabindranath Tagore, her confession that the true story of her life would make a wonderful novel, her anecdote of her uncle who was editor of a newspaper in Lima, O., her immediate assumption that one believes in free love and will presently say something naughty. I always accommodate them. More often than not, my own stuff makes me blush, for I am a poor hand at polite indelicacy and I hate the obvious — but it always seems to please them. Who ever heard of such a miss getting offended when one introduced the sub-motif in F sharp minor? Like every other vain fellow, I delight in shocking the virtuous, but it is a pleasure that I seldom enjoy any more. However, the encounter itself is agreeable enough. A man is an idiot who says that he doesn't like to talk to a pretty girl. It is, perhaps, the most delightful of all imbecilities. I'd leave a performance of Beethoven's Eighth to do it. I'd almost leave a good meal to do it.

Nathan

If, as you observe, a man is an idiot who says that he doesn't like to talk to a pretty girl, put me down at once for an idiot. (*Your sleeve, Gustavus, is in the remains of the Camembert.*) I like a pretty girl as much as anyone, but spare me from talking to her. I have yet to find a pretty girl who understands the technique of silence. Talking to a pretty girl is much like having gazed admiringly for an hour at a beautifully carved Sonora and then suddenly hearing the damned thing play "The Livery

Stable Blues." I'd leave a performance of "Rosenkavalier," or a quart of Chambertin, to *look* at a pretty girl, but surely not to address her.

Mencken

You are eloquent — but you fail to move me. The trouble with *you* is that you don't know what to *say* to a pretty girl.

Nathan

Good Roderigo, I confess it. There is something about a pretty girl that ties this old tongue. I imagine that it's because I can't synchronize my tongue and my eye. I suppose that you, however, your eye fixed immovably by the sudden bursting of a dazzling, multi-coloured sky-rocket, can simultaneously recite Lincoln's Gettysburg address.

Mencken

You suppose wrong. You miss the point. The only way to talk to a pretty girl is to talk nonsense. And I am a virtuoso of nonsense.

Nathan

Say no more, I agree with you perfectly. But we were talking about the theater. You had better come along with me. The play is one of your old friend Ibsen's.

Mencken

What! Ibsen!! Not for ten thousand dollars! Seeing old Heinie in a theater at this late day is like going to a Y.M.C.A. picnic in a cemetery. Make it a burlesque show, and I'll go [*sic*] you.

Nathan

Burlesque is no longer any good. They've taken all the jounce out of it. They've censored out all the old loud jokes, the faded tights, the seltzer siphon, the trouser walloper — everything that made it. Now it's nothing but advanced vaudeville in overalls.

Mencken

Too bad. The theater is essentially a bazaar of vulgarity. To refine it is to kill it as a source of diversion for refined persons.

Nathan

The English are a wiser lot in this regard than we. The King, they say, has lately knighted George Robey, the vulgarest actor on the

Anglo-Saxon stage, and has given the cold shoulder to Charles Hawtrey, the most refined.

Mencken

What pleasure, in God's name, do *you* get out of seeing Ibsen in the theater at this belated hour?

Nathan

Absolutely none.

Mencken

Then why do you go?

Nathan

I don't go to the theater for pleasure, but out of curiosity. Just as I go to Montmartre in Paris, the Tiergarten in Berlin, or to Coney Island in New York. I like to observe how *other* people find pleasure in the theater. This, I believe, is at the bottom of all theater-going. Where could you find a man who would go to a theater if he were given to understand that he would be the only person in the auditorium? A man isn't said "to go to the play": he is said "to go to the theater." The phrase is not accidental; it is exact. He goes less to see a play than a crowd. That's why a circus never in the history of the modern world has failed to play to big business.

Mencken

Your remarks are typically those of a ninth-rate campus snob. You are trying to make me believe that you go to the theater to witness the boobs at their degrading pleasure. The fact is you go there as a boob yourself. The theater is essentially a boob trap. Whenever I went to it in your company it was because alcohol and the persuasive philosophies of such fellows as Brander Matthews, David Belasco, Al Woods and Robert Edmond Jones had reduced me temporarily to the intellectual state of a Presbyterian deacon. No civilized man in a civilized moment ever goes to the theater. If at such a time he feels the need of recreation he goes to hear an orchestra concert or reads a good book — or even a bad book.

Nathan

And again typically, my dear Tewksbury, you seek to make an impression upon me — and upon that good-looking woman at the next table — by sedulously — and rather loudly — evading my point and seizing on another about which you have something saucy to say. Who contends that going to the theater is a pleasure? Only a few moments ago I observed that it was not. You posture, too, when you say that when you are looking for pleasure you go to a symphony concert, or read a good book. You forget that I know you, old tosspot! I know well enough the yokel nature of the pleasures you seek and cherish.

Mencken

You have become in the early years of your senility such a mass of preposterous affectations that it gradually becomes impossible for a man of refined instincts to hold any conversation with you whatever. For example, consider your doctrine that it is not a pleasure to go to the theater. What could be more erroneous? If it is not a pleasure, in God's name what is it? I insist against all your evidences and syllogisms that you yourself go to the theater in search of the precise thing you disdain. In other words, you enjoy the adventure intensely. What is true in your gabble is this: that the sort of pleasure you enjoy is essentially *infra dig*. It differs in degree, but not in kind, from such pleasures as simple men get out of playing golf, engaging each other in bridge combats, reading the New York *Times*, choosing neck-ties, watching circus parades, singing "The Star Spangled Banner," and praying to God. Every man has his moments of weakness and at such moments he turns invariably to that sort of recreation. All I maintain is that my own depravities are measurably superior to those of the theater-goer. If I read a book for pleasure, it's almost invariably a bad book — that is a book condemned by the right-thinking opinion of Christendom. If I engage a pretty creature in conversation, it is surely not for any lofty purpose. If I go to a concert, it is nine times out of ten with the aim of laughing in a superior manner at the idiotic antics of some English composer.

Nathan

You support my argument for me. I go to the theater for precisely the same reason. Surely, as I have already said to you, I do not go to see the plays of such ducks as Ibsen for any amusement that the plays themselves might give me. I derive pleasure from the spectacle precisely as you, in your case, derive pleasure from reading dull books, talking to duller women, and listening to even more stupid English fugues. Although you do not seem to know it, you yourself get the same kind of pleasure, and in exactly the same way, as I. The only difference between us is that you favour a sort of emotional *pas seul*, while I go in for quadrilles.

Mencken

Quod erat demonstrandum. In brief, you agree with me absolutely. What I argue is that theater-going is entirely devoid of intellectual content. You now say the same thing. Nevertheless, I suspect that your mind is still full of some sort of vague notion that the theater is measurably above, say, a Methodist camp-meeting, a chautauqua or a zoological garden. Here, with the highest respect, I believe that you are in error.

Nathan

Your arguments are indirectly so good that they defeat you. You say that you are not going to the theater with me tonight because you find an insufficient pleasure in such an adventure. Yet you sit here and spend the whole evening listening to *my* arguments. That this is a great pleasure, I do not deny. But think, my dear Hugo, what you are missing — what I am missing. The curtain is already up. A two-hundred-and-ten pound Nora is yelling her head off at a Helmer who wears a conspicuously false set of whiskers that are constantly in the act of coming unglued. Meantime, in the neighbourhood of our fauteuils, the ancient critic for the *Evening Post* is screwing up a large frown and giving every evidence of being deeply impressed by the bosh. Now Nora, in a pair of twenty-five dollar Slater slippers, a three-hundred dollar gown from Bendel's and a ruby stomacher, is deploring her sad lot. Again, meanwhile . . .

Mencken

My dominant craving, like that of every other civilized man, is for beauty. How much beauty is in the spectacle you offer? You mention the dramatic critic of some obscure cheese-paper. Think of what the face of such a man must be. Put beside it, the façade of the Elks' Hall at Union Hill, N.J., is a thing of loveliness. Think of the mind behind the face — a mind paralyzed and petrified by fifty, sixty, seventy or eighty years of incessant theater-going. Let us call up Tom Smith and find out if he is still decent enough to invite us to a small glass. I have no more to say.

Nathan

Your last remark comes too late by half an hour. Yet here, once again, you argue in the same channel that I do. It is the very absence of beauty that makes the spectacle inviting. You surely don't contend that Otta Dinkelspiel, a burlesque comedian, or Sidney Blatz, a music-show comedian, must be handsome in order to amuse you. Or a critic for the *Post*. Anyway, Tom Smith is at the very theater I am inviting you to. He is a great Ibsen fan.

Mencken

You mistake me, my poor friend. Certainly I have not maintained that Tom Schmidt is a pretty fellow. I maintain nothing of the kind! He is not even well finished. Have you ever observed the spats he wears? He is the sort of man who would put a heavy band of crêpe around his plug hat to go to the funeral of a marionette. Naturally, I make these remarks confidentially. It would be rather indelicate for me to criticize his personal aspect after having drunk so may carboys of his excellent synthetic wines — and just before drinking, I hope and pray, a few more gallons. My proposal, therefore, is that we engage some public vehicle and proceed at once to the gentleman's chambers. Even if, as you say, he is now polluting his mind with Ibsenism he will return anon and it would surely be a felicitous thing to be waiting in his hallway, as he comes in, to join him in his ten or twelve nightcaps. Let us, I repeat, employ a public hackman to haul us thither.

Nathan

Spero che abbiate abbastanza denaro?

Mencken

Si, ne ho abbastanza.

————————————

Conversation II: "On Anatomy and Physiology"

Scene: *The Smart Set office in 45th Street.*

Time: *An autumn morning.*

Nathan

There is that damned pain in my chest again. Do you think it signifies anything?

Mencken

Where is it?

Nathan

(*Indicating the region of the left supraspinatus muscle.*) Here.

Mencken

That isn't your chest: that's your shoulder.

Nathan

Well, what is the difference *what* it is? A pain is a pain.

Mencken

You probably strained yourself pulling a tight cork, or getting on your undershirt.

(*A pause. Both resume work. Then:*)

Nathan

You don't think there could be any congestion?

Mencken

Where?

Nathan

Well, say in the lungs.

Mencken

What is the evidence?

Nathan

The pain —

Mencken

It isn't in your lungs; it's in your shoulder.

Nathan

I've had a touch of cold since Monday.

Mencken

Is it any wonder? It's a marvel to me that you are alive at all, considering the way you live.

Nathan

What is the matter with the way I live?

Mencken

Almost everything. In the first place, you never get any fresh air whatsoever. I venture to say that on your average day you don't take in six honest lungs full — maybe not even four. Consider your routine. You get up at eight, leap to your bedroom window, pull it down all the way, and then go into a steamy bathroom. Then you go down into the rathskeller of the Royalton and eat your breakfast. Then you walk two blocks to the office, and sit here until lunch-time with the windows closed. And where do you go for lunch? To Delmonico's, or Pierre's, or across the street to the Lorraine, or back to the Royalton — at most, two blocks. Then, after drowsing in the office for another hour or two, you return to the Royalton, pull down the curtains, light one of those amber bordello lamps, and work all afternoon. Then to dinner at some great distance, maybe three blocks — say the Beaux Arts, or the Ritz, or the Crillon. If you go as far as Del Pezzo's or the Hofbräuhaus you take a taxicab — with both windows closed. Then to some theater for two or three hours of pure carbon dioxide. Then to some *cabinet particulier* to drink the poisons of the boot-leggers. A fit life for a mammal? Never in the world! Rather a life for a *Wanze*, or an actor.

Nathan

I keep my bedroom window open.

Mencken

Yes, but what a window! If it's more than thirty-six inches wide, then I give you a free license to throw me out of it. And where is your bed? In the far corner — as far away from the window as you can get it. And *what* a bed — all heavy comforters and satin spreads. It always reminds me of that painting in the Louvre — I think it is called "The Accouchement of Marie Antoinette." You live like a high-class *fille de joie*. No wonder you have colds!

Nathan

(*Ironically.*) I suppose you advise a sleeping-porch — here in New York. Like yours in Baltimore.

Mencken

Of course not. A properly built sleeping-porch is one of the noblest comforts of civilization, and hence impossible in New York. There are no actual comforts in New York; there are only luxuries — and most of them are luxuries designed, not for healthy human beings, but for diabetic fat women.

Nathan

That sleeping-porch of yours fills me with snickers. I can see you sneaking in on cold nights, and —

Mencken

(*Indignantly.*) Never! I *never* come in. I actually have no bed in my house.

Nathan

Well, what is the sense in it? Why freeze?

Mencken

I don't. I have heavy army blankets, and I wear flannel pajamas.

Nathan

Oh, my God! Spare me the flannel pajamas! You probably look like Marie Dressler. I suppose you also wear pulse-warmers!

Mencken

No — and no ear-muffs.

Nathan

Well, the flannel pajamas are enough. I have seen them, pink and lavender, in shop-windows. Suppose you should die in the night, and the coroner should bring his jury in to look at you!

Mencken

(*Maliciously.*) And you? Suppose *you* should die in the night — of one of your imaginary diseases? What would the coroner say when he came into that bedroom of yours — with that thick, green carpet, and all of those feather-pillows? I offer two to one that he'd take one look — and then ask to see the madame.

Nathan

And what of it? Where would a sane man prefer to die — in a comfortable private hotel, or in an open shed?

Mencken

But you miss the point. The point is that the sleeping-porch makes death more unlikely — staves it off — preserves the health.

Nathan

Slobbergobble! Then why doesn't it preserve *your* health?

Mencken

It does. I am —

Nathan

Slobbergobble again! You are a chronic invalid, just as I am. For five years past I can't remember a single day when you didn't complain of some malaise or other. If you haven't got something the matter with your nose or your eyes then you have a ringing in the ears, and if your ears are all right then you have hay-fever, and if it isn't the hay-fever season then you have lumbago. Why, you have been on the operating table at least forty times in five years. Every time you go home to Baltimore you have some sort of operation performed. You must look like a Hamburg steak by this time. It's a wonder to me that you have enough organs left to keep you going.

Mencken

I return your slobbergobble. I am forty years old, and sound in wind and limb. I have never had to have a capital operation. A few minor clippings and borings — that's all. At twenty I was a weakling — ordered to give up all work, and go to the West Indies for my health. I came home much worse, but still on my legs. Meanwhile, the doctor who had advised me to clear out had come down with something or other himself, and presently I went to his funeral. Then I fell into the hands of better doctors — and here I am, fat, healthy and happy.

Nathan

So it was doctors who saved you? I thought it was your sleeping-porch.

Mencken

The two together.

Nathan

But why pay a doctor to advise you to sleep on a sleeping-porch? You could get precisely the same advice from a head-waiter, or a clergyman, or a garbage-hauler — and it wouldn't cost you a cent.

Mencken

You talk nonsense. A sleeping-porch is no cure-all. In fact, it cures nothing. It is a mere precaution against disease — it increases a man's disvulnerability. However hard I work down there in Baltimore, bending over my desk all day, manufacturing literature for an obtuse and abominable peasantry, I always get at least eight hours of fresh air during the twenty-four. That is above the average, even of men who are often outdoors. Give me those eight hours, and I can stand any amount of work during the day. My workroom in Baltimore is hermetically sealed, at least in winter. I try to shut out all disturbing sound. Down there the folks still keep dogs and have children, and both have to be beaten, and are thus noisy. I live, in fact, in a very fecund neighbourhood. I am probably the only man for blocks around without viable issue. Well, raising children is almost as noisy a business as running a nail-factory. They whoop and yell all day. Worse, the general disturbance, the wear and tear on the nerves, sets their parents to quarreling. This constant torture, in fact, is the chief cause of domestic brawls. Have you ever heard of a childless couple who fought each other? It is a common superstition that children tighten the bond between husband and wife, or, as the phrase has it, "hold them together." No doubt you believe it yourself. But it is not true. Even old August Strindberg, an idiot, knew better. Whenever I hear that some young married woman whom I know is expecting, it makes me sad. On the one hand, it is terrible to think of bringing an innocent child into a world filled with Methodists, lawyers, *agents provocateurs*, press-agents, Congressmen, Socialists, Italians, unhappy married women, war veterans —

Nathan

Don't forget long-winded talkers.

Mencken

And on the other hand, there is the ghastly thought that the young one will presently set its pa and ma to hating each other. I have seen it happen over and over again. During the pre-natal period, of course, there is no quarreling, save perhaps for one grand row when the news is broken. A man would feel like a brute to quarrel with his wife at such a time. All his moony sentimentality stands against it — and women always capitalize the fact. The husband's one aim is to prove his chivalry, his native nobility. Many a shrewd woman, I daresay, has deliberately had a child in order to get a grand piano, or a set of furs, or a country place. In fact, I could give you names and dates. But once the poor infant is born, trouble begins. Its generation was a poem — something, say, comparable to a performance of "Tristan und Isolde." But its rearing always turns out to be a vexatious and noisesome business — a match, say, for running an auction-house or driving a pair of mules.

Nathan

But what has all this got to do with you? Surely *you* are not expecting to become a father.

Mencken

God forbid! I'd die of mortification. What I was getting at is this: that eight hours of fresh air in the twenty-four are enough to let me do absolutely as I please during the other sixteen hours. I smoke half a box of cigars — and keep all of the smoke in the room. The air is something fearful. A visitor would faint in ten minutes. You would gag and wheeze like a man with asthma. I never have the same caller twice. Let a stranger come in and begin to talk about Maeterlinck, or *Imagisme*, or Paul Elmer More, and before he can really annoy me, he is strangling, and I have to haul him out. Yet I breathe that flying sediment, that volcanic effluvia, all day — and thrive on it. The answer is that I get enough fresh air at night to last me until the next night. Not only are my lungs full, but also all the other recesses of my body. Compressed air is stored away in my very legs. When I am in New York and have to sleep in a hotel room, I feel half suffocated.

Nathan

All this sounds like piffle to me. If you are so healthy, then why are you always complaining of being ill?

Mencken

You miss the point. I am not intrinsically healthy; I am merely artificially healthy. At the age of twenty I was theoretically ready for the embalmer; at the age of forty I am a first-rate insurance risk, have a low blood pressure, and am able to do all my work. I give the whole credit to sound medical advice. I know a great many medical men, and most of them are very good ones. I have simply put myself in their hands. The fact that I am alive today is a massive proof that modern medicine is shrewd, accurate and a success.

Nathan

I should say that it is rather merely a massive proof that modern medicine is not snobbish.

Mencken

Forgive my not laughing. I have a slight attack of tonsilitis.

Nathan

When, go on with your prattle. You are never happy unless you are talking; and I like to see you have a good time.

Mencken

Thanks. Now then, to go back to what I was saying. I know that what I have said is the truth. All talk to the contrary is simply so much moonshine — especially when it comes from medical men themselves, say in their hours of *Katzenjammer*. It is a common saying that there are only five drugs that are worth a damn; all the rest are dismissed as useless, and even as dangerous. Nothing could be more imbecile. There are at least fifty drugs that are worth a great deal more than a damn — and I include only actual drugs, not antitoxins, vaccines, or anything of that sort. But they must be administered intelligently, scientifically, carefully. The trouble with the average doctor is not that he uses too many drugs, but that he doesn't use enough — that he doses all his patients with one or two of them. The layman usually falls into the same error. Think of the number of diseases that quinine is taken for — and yet quinine is useful in malaria only, and in nothing else. As for me, I seldom swallow a dose of medicine, and never without medical advice — never so much as a liver pill. If I feel ill for a day or two, I do absolutely nothing. Nine times out of ten recovery follows as soon as I have caught up with my lost sleep, or sweated out my overdose of alcohol, or got over having slept in a hotel.

Nathan

And what is the sum of all this jabber? That I, who sleep in a comfortable, warm bed in a comfortable, warm room, and haven't a single doggoned theory pro or con, have actually been laid up only one week in the last twelve years — when I had the flu. And that you, who wear pink flannel pajamas, shiver yourself to sleep *al fresco*, and are kept busy living up to your innumerable hypotheses, are no better off than I am. Not so *well* off. The fresh-air thing is largely buncombe. The healthiest labourers, for example, are coal miners. And don't tell me that they get plenty of fresh air at night, since they live in the open country. I've seen where they live. And how they live. So have you. Even if they slept with their one window open, which they don't, they'd breathe in the day's residuum of dirt, coal dust, smoke, bed clothing, and pieces of the Pittsburgh *Dispatch*.

Mencken

But don't forget that they get a lot of exercise.

Nathan

I don't. Nor do I forget that professional baseball players get a lot of exercise — to say nothing of a lot of fresh-air — and that a baseball player of fifty who isn't a physical wreck is as rare as an uncooked lamb chop.

Mencken

They're wrecks, not because of the exercise or the fresh air, but because of dissipation after hours.

Nathan

Rot! Dissipation is the eternal Patsy Bolivar. Everything is blamed on dissipation. Yet dissipation, I daresay, has little to do with health one way or another. Take ourselves, for instance. In the old drinking days, we'd sit up until three in the morning consuming one seidel after another and one Invincibilia Greco Splenderoso Superbo after another, all the while mellowly devising and planning books, plays, magazines, pamphlets, what not. And the next morning at nine we'd be at our desks in high shape working like the devil. We were well, happy, accomplishing things. Now we sit around until midnight sucking ginger ale, smoking an appropriately weak cigar or two, revamping stale ideals, getting nowhere, and — the next morning — come down full of marble dust, dispirited, sick.

Mencken

There, my friend, you fetch a torpedo! There is nothing so good for one as intelligent alcoholization. I am surely not what any sane man would call a booze-master. I drink all I want, and maybe ten per cent more, but I seldom want enough to shake me up. Now and then I like to get quietly stewed, but that is all. I often go four or five days without a single drink, as you know, but do not quite believe. Nevertheless, I firmly and honestly believe, as I hope to sit upon the right hand of Jehovah when I die, that a certain amount of alcohol is absolutely necessary to my welfare, and even to my existence. My ancestors have been alcoholics for thirty generations. I could no more do without the stuff than I could do without *Linsensuppe*, or vitamins, or oxygen. I get along all right for days and days, but finally there comes a moment when I must have a seidel of malt or bust.

Nathan

At last you are exuding sense. When you do it, I don't mind listening to you, even though I can't listen and correct the infernal spelling in this book review of yours at one and the same time. Go on, my dear professor. *Da capo.*

Mencken

You recall the immortal words of Paul, *geb.* Saul, in Timothy V, 23: "Noli adhuc aquam bibere, sed modico vino utere propter stomachum tuum et frequentes tuas infirmitates." The dear fellow probably goes a bit too far. "Noli adhuc aquam bibere" is laying it on rather thick. As for me, I drink a great deal of water — perhaps ten quarts a day. It prevents diabetes, the great curse of the literati. My great-grandfather, Prof. Dr. Giuseppe da Mencken, never touched water after the age of twenty-one. He even had his coffee boiled in Pinot Chardonay [*sic*]. He died at thirty-eight.

Nathan

Nevertheless —

Mencken

But, as you say, Paul was right in his main contention. You and I are physical wrecks. All I have to do is to shut my eyes and I can feel the embalmer's squirt-gun sticking into my flank. We suffer from "frequentes infirmitates." *Ergo*, we need an occasional hooch for our stomachs', but also for our livers', kidneys', spleens', lungs' and gizzards'.

Nathan

You mentioned malt liquor. Can it be that in Baltimore —

Mencken

Even so.

Nathan

But —
(*They whisper.*)
Is it possible?

Mencken

Last week I drank twenty-nine seidels — all free. Not a cent to pay. They are glad to make you happy.

Nathan

But tell me —
(*They whisper.*)

Mencken

As I say, gin is a different question. But the other day a friend of mine at the Johns Hopkins —
(*They whisper.*)

Nathan

But what of vermouth?
(*They whisper.*)

Mencken

You know, of course, that red wine ought to be at least a year old before —
(*They whisper.*)

Nathan

Let me take down his address.

Mencken

Give the name of Mr. Farley.

Nathan

But I thought —
(*They whisper.*)

Mencken

I wouldn't touch such stuff for —
(*They whisper.*)

Nathan

Well, when I emptied the last bottle I —
(*They keep on whispering.*)
[Curtain]

————————————

Conversation III: "On Women"

Scene: *An automobile on the way to Longue Vue.*

Mencken

That gal in the lavender frock standing on the steps of yonder chateau takes my eye. She is pretty, and she looks intelligent.

Nathan

It is the lavender frock, not the gal, that is pretty. You have arrived at an age where any woman wearing a colour other than black fetches you. That yon chicken looks intelligent, I do not gainsay. But why admire intelligence in a pretty woman? Does one ask that a Corot landscape be intelligent? Does one itch to have a song by Brahms stimulate one's thoughts to speculations on basal metabolism, the theory of relativity, or the elimination of urticaria following injections of horse-serum? Simple beauty should be enough for any man. You are a hog.

Mencken

And you, my dear Confucius, are an acousticon. Why do you like female morons? Very simply, because they give you an opportunity to unload your repertoire of ponderous pishposh on them without shooting you in the eye with a pêche Melba, as an intelligent woman would.

Nathan

You are only half right, old seidel. Woman, as I see her, is a spectacle, not a chautauqua. Intelligence ruins a pretty woman, as intelligence ruins a pretty musical show.

Mencken

Intelligence does nothing of the sort. It is impossible for a sheer bonehead to be pretty. A pretty baby with a noodle crammed with nothing but air is like a beautiful sausage skin without any Frankfurter in it.

Nathan

We differ for a plain reason. What you seek in a girl is stimulation. What I seek is rest. When I want stimulation I drink half a dozen cocktails. They're quicker — and cheaper.

Mencken

I don't seek stimulation in a woman: I seek recreation. And I can't find recreation unless my vis-à-vis has some sagacity. Beauty is not enough.

Nathan

What can be more recreative than that very beauty? Did you ever need a woman to hold your hand when your eyes were regaled by the beauty of the Austrian Tyrol or by the Champs Élysées in the spring when the yellow nightlights are on, or by a long blue-white stretch of sea and sand? Didn't you find a greater companionship in this beauty than in any intelligent woman you ever met, and bought a bad dinner for?

Mencken

The answer is no. The more I ponder the great problems of being and becoming, the more I am convinced that mere pulchritude is dross. I have known in my time some very sightly damsels, and one or two of them have fallen for my blather and been at pains to be polite to me. But I remember them only visually, as spectacles without substance or significance, and, as you know, my sight is the least sensitive of all my five senses. I am, for one thing, almost colour blind. In my youth I acquired painfully, as one acquires table manners and the multiplication table, the news that certain colours clash — that no gentleman ever wears a purple tie with a blue shirt. But beyond that I have never gone. Stand me before a colour combination that is new to me, and I am flabbergasted. That is why I always wear blue clothes, blue shirts and blue cravats. They match my eyes and set off my ruddy, sclerotic complexion.

All women regard me as a tasty fellow. The blue monotone somehow pleases them. They attach a psychic significance to it, and so think that I am blue internally, which also pleases them, for they like a sad boy — one who knows how to sigh. But the combination is really no more than a sort of refuge or trade-mark. Some men roll their eyes all the time, or talk business all the time, or are stewed all the time. I am simply in blue all the time.

Nathan

But you evade the issue. We are not discussing your personal beauty, but the beauty of the innumerable caravan of enterprising and ever-amusing females. What I dispute is your doctrine that pulchritude is not enough, that a pretty girl is not her own sufficient excuse for existence. Here, my dear Herr Kollege, you wander into metaphysical piffle. What joy could be more delicate than purely æsthetic joy? And where is that joy to be found in greater measure than in the presence of young and lovely women? Nothing else is half so beautiful — not the finest score of old Ludwig, or the finest canvas of Rembrandt, or the most purple passage in the old dramatists. I delight in gaping at pretty wenches.

Mencken

It is your calamity. It explains why you are so easily intrigued by what you call morons. I have often observed you with melancholy. There was, for example, that fair creature you met in Paris in 1917 — the girl from Youngstown, Ohio, whose father broke his leg in the Hotel Continental. A lovely sight, I grant you — under glass. But what a mind! Apply the Binet-Simon test to such a blockhead and the indicator will show that she is less than one year old — in fact, that she will not be born until next December a year.

Nathan

Perhaps. But I didn't admire her mind. I admired her externally — her complexion, her eyes, her hair, her youth.

Mencken

Youth, youth! What a delusion! You were born senile. You show all of an old man's pathetic delight in mere youngness. To all of that I am anæsthetic. The women that you admire are, roughly speaking, about half the age of those that I admire. What puzzles me is this: why do you stop at twenty? If a girl of twenty, as you say, is twice as charming as a woman of forty, then a child of ten should be twice as charming as a girl of twenty.

Nathan

It sometimes is. I like children. They are naïve and often amusing — in a Rabelaisian way.

Mencken

And always ignorant, stupid, selfish and piggish. Children should be confined in public institutions. They feed upon flattery. They make intolerable noises. They smell badly. They are devoid of humour. Describe a child, and you have described a Socialist. If God blessed me with a child tomorrow, I'd sell it for a mess of pottage.

Nathan

See Freud, chapter ten, verse sixteen. You are talking nonsense. Worse, it is nonsense with a sinister inner meaning. You are actually a good family man gone to waste. You should have married at twenty-five and gone in for raising cannon-fodder. I never knew a more domestic man. The things you admire in women are not the attributes of a pretty girl, but those of a middle-aged multipara. You lately confided to me that you wear flannel pajamas on your sleeping-porch in Baltimore. I venture to say that you could almost bring yourself to admire a woman who wore flannel nightgowns.

Mencken

Bah! You betray one of the weaknesses of your case. What you admire in a woman is the clothes rather than the woman. Young girls wear bright colours, and so they take your eye. You constantly remind me of a small boy following a circus band-wagon. Let the gal be flashy enough, and you succumb instantly. Mine is chiefly aural: I judge them by what they say, and by the tone in which they say it. Clang-tint is what fetches me. I could never resist a girl with a low and musical voice.

Perhaps that is why I am so exogamous. The American woman pitches her voice too high.

Mencken [*sic*]

That is American credo No. 762. The shrillest voices are those of French woman. If the voice is the true test, then my coloured char-woman, Mrs. Evelyn Jones, is the loveliest creature in New York. She has a superb *Bierbass*. I often listen with delight as she mops up my bathroom singing, "Oh, How I Love Jesus." But as for me, I think she is too fat.

Mencken

Excuse me. I am a Southerner, and hate all coons, however meritori-ous. In fact, the more meritorious they are, the more I am bound to hate them. No Southern idealist ever objects to a Moor who is poor, shift-less, ignorant, ragged and spiritless. What he objects to is the Moor who begins to show dignity, efficiency and self-respect. Thus I am permitted to admire Mrs. Jones as a charwoman, but forbidden to admire her as a vocalist. Let her sing so beautifully that she reduces you to sobs, I must nevertheless maintain that she has the voice of a Follies girl.

Nathan

Even so. But which would you rather look at, a Follies girl or Schumann-Heink? You say that my eyes deceive me, that let a girl make up like a plate of French pastry and at once I hear the coo of angels in her voice and the gurgle of philosophers in her discourse. You seek to tangle up the issue, and save your own face. It is, as I have said, of no moment to me whether a girl has a voice like a second-hand trombone or the mind of a flagpole painter, so long as she is pretty enough, and keeps her mouth shut. My eye is interested in neither elocution nor pro-fundity. *You* look at a woman through your ears. Which is like looking at perfume or smelling music.

Mencken

You are reduced to sneers. My syllogisms fetch you.

Nathan

They fetch me exactly as I am fetched by ipecacuanha.

Mencken

(*Suddenly leaning halfway out of the automobile.*)
There! There!

Nathan

(*Peering through the rear window.*)
Where? Which one?

Mencken

The one with the yellow hat.

Nathan

O mon Dieu! *That?* I saw her before you did — a decrepit old baggage. She is thirty-four if she is a day.

Mencken

Well, what of it? Are you so steeped in darkness that you are unaware that a handsome woman reaches her maximum between thirty and thirty-five. At the moment, I can't recall ever encountering a woman under thirty who was genuinely worth looking at.

Nathan

Spare me the details! I may burglarize the nursery, as you say, but I at least avoid the dissecting-room.

Mencken

Your tastes remain crude and untutored. You like the gross, lush beauty of youth — the beauty of a dahlia in full bloom. When you are as old as I am, and have seen as much of the world, and suffered and sorrowed as much, you will begin to realize that beauty is at its best at the moment it is first touched by decay — that the rose showing a petal that has begun to shrivel is infinitely more delicate and lovely than all the dahlias in all the funeral wreaths at all the Odd Fellows' funerals ever pulled off. So with a woman. The thing that makes her perfect is the first appearance of fine lines around the eyes. They give her a touch of melancholy — and melancholy is absolutely essential to the highest sort of beauty. Why is a melody by Schubert the most beautiful thing ever devised by man? Because there is always wistfulness in it. The lady who has begun to oxidize has the same ineffable charm. She is perfect, and she is transient. She won't last, and she knows it. This sense of mortality is what gives women their final charm. The young girl is simply unable to imagine her own decay. The egoism of youth protects her. Hence she may be pretty, but she can never be romantic. But an oldish gal who spends a sad hour before her mirror every morning, gently cursing God — a fully adult creature whose heart has begun to be aware of that ominous sinking, that far-away and gaseous feeling, that sensation of rats gnawing at the soul — this is the one for Henry. The beauty of such a woman often grows almost transcendental. She seems to carry with her an aura of downright ghostliness. She is as romantic as the Acropolis, or "Heart of Darkness," or the slow movement of Schumann's Rhenish Symphony. And her conversation is shot through with the same profound and charming melancholy. What could be more beautiful than to talk to such a woman? One stands fascinated before her gentle disillusionment, her resigned agnosticism. An hour with her is as fascinating as an hour of Eighteenth Century music.

Nathan

And as depressing. I prefer the *scherzo* to the *largo*. My everyday life is such a curse, what with my incessant malaises, my enormous expenses and the harsh need to labour, that I like the women I meet to be gay. Give me a jolly cutie, and I'll let you have all your Acropolises. I don't ask a woman to stimulate me to lofty reflection; even purely æsthetic reflection is too much. All I ask is that she entertain my eye, and divert my thoughts from my troubles. You say that you view women as recreations. Well, what recreation can there be in contemplating the gradual oxidation of an eyeball, the conversion of a soft pink skin into a leather of unstable colloids, the slow curing of a head of hair, as hops and tobacco are cured? If you regard that sort of thing as charming, then all I can say is that you are morbid, and should put your feet into a wine-bucket of mustard-water before retiring. Could one dance with such a pessimist as you depict? Or take her to a roof-show? Or give her a buss behind the ear in a taxicab?

Mencken

Your notions grieve me greatly. Give sober heed to your own words! What sort of ideal do you hold up? What is the kind of joy-in-women that you describe? It is, in every detail, precisely and exactly the kind that is sought by a moving-picture actor or a curb-broker.

Nathan

In God's name, no! The joy-in-women that I describe is rather precisely and exactly the kind that is sought by an intelligent man on a holiday. You can get tired of your frequent railroad trips to Baltimore, your 1906 Panama hat, the bust of Louisa M. Alcott in your workroom, your purple socks, escaloppes of veal à la Creole, your hay-fever. I, on the other hand, simply get tired of my intelligence.

Mencken

But how does your intelligence get a vacation with the kind of girl you describe? If I sat down with that kind it would take all my intelligence to reconcile me to the abject depths to which I had permitted myself to sink. Intelligence is diverted only by intelligence. Imagine an intelligent man finding abstraction on a merry-go-round!

Nathan

Very well. Go on. I have imagined it.

Mencken

Go back to the question of the moving-picture actor and the curb-broker. What is your idea of what such dolts seek in woman, since you appear to disagree with me?

Nathan

It is impossible for an imbecile like a moving-picture actor or curb-broker to be a connoisseur of that imbecility of woman that is responsible for so much of her charm. Only an intelligent man can accurately and sympathetically appreciate such imbecility, as only a practiced critic of the theater can accurately and sympathetically appreciate the art of such tomfoolery as George Bickel's. The ignoramus sees in a pretty moron only a pretty moron. The student sees in her the highest of all the feminine arts, the art of artlessness. That it is not voluntary, nor a consciously achieved art, doesn't matter. Helen Green didn't know she was creating literature when she set down literally the imbecilities of imbecile telephone girls and vaudevillians, nor did the ignoramuses who read her. In the same way —— —— is a literary artist. If I ever set her ignorance and imbecility literally down on paper, it will be her ignorance and imbecility that will be literature. I'll be merely the recorder. It will be her own lack of ideas and lack of intelligence that will produce the work of art, not I.

Mencken

In other words, you now proceed to flapdoodle — the inevitable refuge of a man worsted in argument. Surely you don't ask me to accept all that fol-de-rol about raw materials being literature as serious doctrine, to be weighed gravely. I hope you respect my years too much to unload any such hokum on me in sober earnest. I tell you in all friendship that you ought to drink more. You are suffering from alcohol starvation, and the fact is showing itself in your mental processes. As you know, I am a particular believer in the virtues of malt liquor. I drink every drink known, and have secret means of obtaining all of them even today, but I am thoroughly convinced that malt does me more good than any other — that the rest are merely luxuries and dissipations, whereas malt is as necessary to me as honey to the bee or hell to the Christian. Take it away from me, and I'd gradually subside to the level of an ordinary literary snob.

Nathan

I hope I do not offend you when I opine that many of your failings are due to the overuse of malt — for example, your sentimentality. You have, with all possible respect, a somewhat beery mind.

Mencken

You don't offend me. I admit it. More, I am glad of it. It has brought me happiness.

Nathan

And purple socks. Nevertheless —

Mencken

I'll come to that in a moment. What I desire to say now is that even the large and refined delight that I take in feminine society is principally due to malt. Women who are genuinely intelligent are very rare in such societies as you and I frequent. Your reaction to the fact you have described: that is, you observe them as idiots, and have convinced yourself that they are amusing as idiots. My own reaction is different. Before I engage an unknown woman in conversation, I drink a few *Humpen* of malt. The result is invariable, and very agreeable. A veil rises before my eyes, and through it she appears to be not only beautiful, but also sagacious. Even when she begins to quote Arthur Brisbane, Walter Pater and Nietzsche, I am delighted. Thus I enjoy feminine society much more than you do, both qualitatively and quantitatively, and my sum of happiness is much augmented. In the same way, and for the same reason, I enjoy Italian opera more than you do. If I drank well-water and then went to hear "Traviata," I'd burst into laughter and be thrown out of the opera-house, an obviously unpleasant experience. As it is, I drink half a case of ale, applaud, and am popular and happy.

Nathan

In brief, it is better to be beery and happy than sober and full of sorrow. You have never grown up. You still spout Omar Khayyam, very badly done into prose.

Mencken

Not at all. The antithesis is fallacious. It is not between being beery and being sober, but between being beery and being bad-ginny or worse-vinous. One must drug one's self somehow to bear life at all — that is, in New York.

Nathan

What a mind to become drugged on 2 per cent lager! Why not try lemon pop, or Moxie?

The Chauffeur

Here you are, gents.
(*They climb out.*)

————————————

Conversation IV: "On Politics"

Scene: *The steps of St. Patrick's Cathedral.*
Time: *2.30 A.M.*

Mencken

You should take more interest in politics. It would —

Nathan

I stopped here to rest, not to be insulted.

Mencken

I mean it seriously.

Nathan

As always. Seriousness is your worst vice. You are the sort of man who would be serious at his own wedding, even at his own hanging.

Mencken

Oh, by no means. I —

Nathan

Well, then, think what you ask. You ask me to take a serious interest in the doings of a crowd of low thieves and mountebanks down at Washington — a parcel of men almost wholly devoid of truth, decency or honour. It is precisely as if you asked me to take a serious interest in the doings of a union of piano-movers over in Long Island City. I decline to pollute my mind with such obscenities.

Mencken

As usual, you fail to fathom my doctrine. What boggles you is the word "serious," inserted by yourself. I by no means ask you to take politics seriously. On the contrary, I commend politics to you as perhaps the most indelicate and amusing show now on view in Christendom —

certainly a damned sight more naughty and rib-sticking than any of the lascivious shows you see along Broadway. I went all the way to San Francisco to see the late Democratic National Convention — eight solid days on the train, a truly horrible journey. Yet I was well repaid, I assure you — quite as well as the Methodist deacons who used to walk eighteen miles to see a decayed Midway girl do the hoochie-coochie in the altogether. The taste for the indecent is universal to man. What is more, it is one of the few tastes that never wears out: all it ever does is to change its terms. When I was young, I liked leg-shows, but that was long, long ago. Today I am anæsthetic to them. I honestly get no joy out of them. I'd just as lief go to an Ibsen play or the Lake Mohonk Conference. But politics still fetches me. It is incredibly gross, Rabelaisian, vulgar, lewd, shocking and revolting. It reminds me, in its general outlines, of the rough clinics in morbid anatomy that used to be pulled off in water-front bordellos in the days before Josephus converted every sailor into a Freudian case. It makes me laugh like the devil. More, it stimulates my patriotism. I thank God that I am an American, and thus admitted to such barbaric saturnalias. In a genuinely civilized country politics would be prohibited by law, and all politicians would be treated like pickpockets or street-walkers. But here they are honoured and prosperous, and so they perform, and I enjoy the peculiar buffoonery that is to my taste.

Nathan

I give you full privilege to go on enjoying it. But spare this old gray head! I can see nothing enjoyable in riding on the steam cars for eight days to look at a thousand idiots who believe that the way to pick out the best man for President of the United States is to rip off their undershirts, tote around banners labelled "O You Kid," sing "Ach, Du Lieber Augustin," squirt tobacco juice on the chairs, and periodically yell "three cheers for Kansas!" Compared with such a spectacle, the leg-show that you decry is a masterpiece of diversion. I would rather look at a pretty leg once than at Henry Cabot Lodge twice — any day. And I'd rather listen to a chorus girl warbling "Kiss Me On the Ear, Gus,

My Mouth Is Full of Gum" than to a suffragette reciting the virtues of General Wood. No, my boy, you have your values mixed. You have told me in the past that you get more pleasure sleeping out of doors in a flannel nightgown, and freezing your knees, than snoozing in a comfortable warm bedroom, and that you get more pleasure talking Futurism to a forty year old baggage than chirping to a twenty year old peppermint. *Now* you tell me that you get more pleasure looking at William Jennings Bryan than at Ann Pennington. Next, I suppose you will inform me that you'd rather kiss Dreiser than Mary Garden.

Mencken

Never! Kiss Dreiser? It's all I can do to *look* at Dreiser! However, you evade the issue. We are not discussing anatomy, but politics. You miss a lot.

Nathan

I miss a lot of imbecile statements mouthed by a lot of jackasses in behalf of a candidate who is generally a lot more of a blockhead than they. I miss reading a lot of tripe about a lot of fourth-rate micks busying themselves with the noble enterprise of getting a third-rate job for a second-rate mick. I miss seeing democracy behind the scenes in its dressing-room, clad only in its chemise. I have no taste for such vulgarity. I prefer a good dog fight.

Mencken

You prefer a dog fight simply because you've never seen such a spectacle as that in San Francisco. Have you, for example, ever seen a United States Senator, pickled to the ears, making an indignant speech on the League of Nations to three traveling salesmen in the lobby of the St. Francis, the foresaid traveling gents being named, respectively, Winckhauser, Eiersalat and Schnitzberger? You have not. Have you, for example, ever seen a candidate for the Presidency, boiled to the eyebrows, try to make an impression on the newspaper correspondents, grab the edge of a table to steady himself and, missing it, land plum on his *Sitzfleisch*? You have not. I repeat, you miss a lot.

Nathan

But you are not describing politics; you are describing Robie's Crack-erjack Burlesquers. I prefer to get such a show at first hand, not a cheap imitation. Why travel eight days on the choo-choo, at a cost of several hundred dollars, to see something that you can see done much better at the Olympic Theater in Fourteenth Street for seventy-five cents?

Mencken

Great God, but you are obtuse! You seem to be quite unaware of the nature of the comic. Its essence is the sharp contrast between dignity and ignominy — the sudden transition from self-satisfaction and im-portance to disaster and discomfiture. In other words, it depends upon leading its victim into a situation wherein all his habitual pretenses are brought to naught. On the stage the thing has to be managed by pretending that the comic actor is really someone of consequence — a boozy king, a rascally grand vizier, the owner of Krausmeyer's flats, a rich push-cart kike, a gaudy coon, a member of Parliament, or some-thing of the sort. Thus one laughs when he kicks the hat with the brick under it, or is caught by his wife kissing a chorus girl, or is beaten at epigrams by the child actor. But all the while, one's pleasure is pumped-up and unsatisfactory, for one knows that the fellow is really only a mummer, and hence a brother to the ox. In politics the clowns are real. One sees the slapstick bounce upon the pantaloons, not of poor rogues and vagabonds, but of United States Senators, governors of great states, Ambassadors, and even Presidents.

Nathan

Nevertheless, they are also brothers to the ox, just as much as the zanies in the Robie show. If, in the pursuit of ribald humour, I have to imagine for the time being that some burlesque ham is the Count de Roquefort, owner of the Trouville Casino, *you* in turn have to imagine that some quondam shyster lawyer from Mead's Pond or Saukville is a purple toga'd Marc Antony with a soupçon of Roman in his soul. The clowns of politics, in good truth, are less real than the clowns of the stage. Which, for example, is the more convincing: William H. Crane's

United States Senator or Hoke Smith's? You exude the platitude that the essence of humour is the sharp contrast between dignity and importance on the one hand and disaster and ignominy on the other. Well, old skeezicks, where is the dignity and importance of your politician? Nowhere but in your own mind, exactly as is the case of the stage actor. In order to pave the way for a good loud belly-laugh, I pretend to myself that Russ Whytal, say, is a millionaire steel magnate and a close confidant of the King of England, while you pretend to yourself that a United States Ambassador to a great European capital is a sagacious statesman and diplomat, and not — as he more often actually is — merely an American who can wear a silk hat without looking like a French hack driver, who can stand on a polished hard-wood floor without slipping, and who has learned how to say "This soup is delicious" in two foreign languages. The platform at your San Francisco convention is just a much a stage as the platform in my Olympic Theater in Fourteenth Street. . . . Do you seriously maintain that the Governor of, say, Arkansas or Iowa is not necessarily an ass?

Mencken

I maintain nothing of the sort. So far as I know, 95 per cent of all politicians are idiots. The very desire for public office is an evidence of imbecility. It is like aspiring to be the supreme exalted archon of the Knights of Pythias, or the grand marshal of the firemen's parade, or a social favourite in Altoona, Pa., or the editor of the leading daily in the Texas Panhandle. Such ambitions are inconceivable to a man of sound taste and genuine self-respect.

Nathan

Well, then, if 95 per cent of them are idiots, where is the fun in watching them swell themselves up and explode? In Matteawan perhaps 95 per cent of the incarcerated idiots also imagine themselves Senators, Governors, and Ambassadors. If you get amusement out of that sort of thing, why not go out there? — it takes only an hour on the train.

Mencken

One moment. What I desire to point out to you is that this intrinsic inferiority of the politician is not reflected in his public position — that under a democracy he is accepted quite gravely as the sapient and important man that he pretends to be, and that he usually deceives himself into believing quite honestly that he is. In other words, his position differs materially from that of the actor, who is regarded with loathing by everyone, including especially all other actors. This is not true of politicians. They are viewed with the highest respect by the mob, by themselves and by other politicians. The mob regards the Governor of Tennessee, say, as a far more important man than Cabell, or Borglum, or even Brahms. In the yet higher ranks of politicians it sees something almost superhuman. Two or three years ago, for example, it was seriously argued by his *pediculæ* that Woodrow Wilson was half-divine — a sort of latter day Messiah in spats, with an eye for an ankle, and two gold teeth. His whole politics began to take on a tone of revelation. He issued his balderdash with the air of Moses on Sinai, nay, of Jaaveh on Sinai. It was obvious that he held himself to be a cut above such second-raters as Mark, Matthew, Luke, and Deuteronomy. And then —

Nathan

And then a couple of stage-hands closed him in "one." But, for all that, I can't see that your argument has anything to do with the case. The circumstance that a politician is gravely accepted by three or four hundred thousand nanny-goats as the sage that he pretends to be, and that he deceives himself in the same direction, surely doesn't make him any better material for a cultivated man's risibilities than a mere stage anticker. There were just as many saps who believed that Richard Mansfield was a Great Intellectual and Great Master as there were saps who believed that Woodrow was a Gladstone and Bismarck. The mob may, as you say, regard a Governor of Tennessee as a more important man than Cabell, or Borglum, or even Brahms, but the same mob in turn regards Charlie Chaplin as a more important man than a Governor of Tennessee — and I'm not certain that, here at least, the mob isn't partly right. Carrying out your argument to its logical conclusion, Elihu Root, whom several hundred thousand Americans soberly consider a Sophocles, is by that fact, and that fact solely, a droller dill pickle than Raymond Hitchcock, whom the same number of Americans openly consider a clown. When I seek humour, I put on my hat and take a short cut. You go to all the trouble of filling up a three-gallon demijohn, laying in a two weeks' supply of shaving cream and tooth power, packing a trunk, booking a long railroad passage, and then spending eight days looking out of the window at Firestone Tire signs.

Mencken

You say that a couple of stage-hands closed in on Woodrow. You don't go far enough. A whole herd of comedians came out, and beat him to a jelly with long strings of Deerfield sausages. With a loud sob he fell out of Heaven backwards, landing on his cofferdam. The heart of the world was broken — and the coccyx of Woodrow. The thing had humour, massive and incomparable humour. This, in brief, is what I always find in politics. I snicker when I observe the politician swelling up and rolling his eye: I know that the seltzer-siphon is being loaded behind the scenes. And I yell with delight when its appalling stream fetches him in the kishgish. Such is my taste in the droll.

Nathan

(*Settling himself in his overcoat and leaning back against the main door of the Cathedral.*) A vulgar show, but I grant it a certain rough jocosity. However, you have to wait too long for your laugh. It is often years between the time a politician begins to swell up and the time the gas is let out of him. In Woodrow's case it took ten years.

Mencken

You underestimate the powers of the human mind — for example, its power of prevision. The fun starts immediately the idiot begins to swell. At that very instant the trained imagination is already capable of picturing his ultimate downfall, and so the show is on. I got a great deal of joy out of Woodrow at the time he was horning into Olympus. I could shut my eyes and see the hail of liver-puddings flying through the air. He was marked for his disaster as plainly as a man with ten per cent of sugar is marked for death. I have trained myself to savour such situations.

Nathan

I am too old to be trained in any such art. It would be difficult to train me to do what even sea-lions and elephants do — for instance, stand on my head or catch a rubber-ball in a crab-net. Fortunately, my capacity for enjoying humour in the theater is congenital. I was born with a taste for it. In my third year, when I was taken to see the Beef Trust Burlesquers for the first time, I yelled so loudly that the family doctor put me to bed and dosed me with aloes. When I was four years old I witnessed Johnnie Ray in "A Hot Old Time," and Robert Mantell in "King Lear." Each brought me down with spasms; they had to stop my mirth with hypnotics. For this talent I claim no credit. I merely mention it as proof that it would be silly for me to waste years trying to acquire a talent for laughing at politicians. The thing would be just as insane as for Beethoven to give up music, and devote ten or twenty years to learning how to paint on china . . . but the hour is late. Is there a taxicab in sight?

Mencken

A moment and I am done. What I further maintain is that the humour of politics belongs to a distinctly higher category that the humour of the burlesque show, not only because the comedians are real men and more eminent than actors, but also because the spectators take a hand in the performance. One gets an even more exalted joy out of the seltzer-siphoning of these spectators than one gets out of the slap-sticking of the principals. Consider, for example, the fate of the millions who honestly believed in Woodrow in the days of his annunciation. Think of their touching faith in his gaudy pishposh — their faith that he would liberate them from capitalist oppression, and put an end to war, and make them all secure and happy, and turn all of the beatitudes into amendments to the Constitution, with a hard-boiled Volstead Act behind every one of them! Think of that dog-like confidence, that colossal credulity, and then that herculean sell! It was almost Greek. It gave a new dignity to democracy. It lifted the thing to classical heights. Euripides never imagined anything more stupendous.

Nathan

Perhaps not. But Euripides knew how to get his ideas over without torturing his audience. In order to enjoy the show you describe, you had to submit to innumerable intolerable inconveniences. You had to read the New York *Times* every day for two or three years. You had to wade through Woodrow's proclamations to the boobery. You had to flay your reason with the *Congressional Record*. And in the end you had to go to Chicago and half sweat to death, and then go to San Francisco and let George Sterling poison you with wood alcohol. All the while, I was quietly roosting here in New York, devoting myself to literature, tasty booze, and the chatter of amusing wenches. To this day I don't know just what it was that Woodrow promised to do for the poor jakes, or why they fell on him with bladders. To this day I haven't the slightest notion what the League of Nations is about. To me it sounds like the title of a movie staged by D. W. Griffith. When I hear it mentioned by some song-writer or boot-legger in the lobby of a theater, there comes up in my mind a picture of two thousand supers in rope whiskers and faded kimonos galloping across a Los Angeles dump made up to resemble the field of Philippi. What in hell do I care if there is a League of Nations or no League of Nations? I am not a movie director.

Mencken

Yet I see you looking through the newspapers every day.

Nathan

(*Yawning.*) But surely not the political parts. I haven't read a news-paper editorial since the year of the Nan Patterson case. I read the head-lines on the murders, inform myself as to the latest developments in boot-legging, take a glance at the scandals, and then work up to a good loud laugh with the dramatic criticisms. All political news I skip, as I skip all ecclesiastical news, marriage notices, society doings, baseball reports and Lost Vigour ads.

Mencken

There's a taxi in the distance! I can see its lights!

Nathan

That's not a taxi; that's the Hotel Gotham.

Mencken

Well, then, let's walk.

Nathan

Come on. But let's light up first. Give me one of those six cent Pittsburgh pickles.

Mencken

(*Handing him one.*) No wonder I am a poor man.

(*They light up, stretch, and move down the Avenue.*)

————————————

Conversation V: "On Literature"

Scene: *The Lackawanna Ferry-slip at Jersey City.*
Time: *Four o-clock of a Winter afternoon.*

Nathan

My objection to literary men is very simple. Nine-tenths of those that I meet are plainly balmy.

Mencken

And what could be more natural than that literary gents *should* be balmy? Can you imagine any pursuit more likely to rot a man's reason? You and I get a taste of the process, though we are not literary gents, but *entrepreneurs* who follow literature as a vice, as other *entrepreneurs* follow golf, cards, the bootleggers, or the wives of yet other *entrepreneurs*. Nevertheless, during the hours when we condescend to practice the art of letters we are, to all intents and purposes, indistinguishable from the professionals, and so become privy to their joys and sorrows. What a hell of a way to serve God! Think of the agony of literary endeavour! A man sitting there in his room *all alone!* He can't admit his friends. He can't have a gal to sit upon his knee. He can't call in musicians to play for him. No, he must sit there absolutely *a cappella*, and wrestle damnably with shy and recalcitrant ideas — things of the lowest conceivable low visibility — wraiths that puff out and vanish every time he thinks he has them by the tail. Who could imagine a more depressing avocation, a more grisly and demoralizing avocation, an avocation more fraught with hazards to the higher cerebral centers, the seat of the faculties, the very soul itself? Literary men are not only imbeciles; they are also usually scoundrels. Is it any wonder?

Nathan

You are eloquent. You move me. You have been at the hole in the beer-keg again.

Mencken

Again? Is it unnatural? I have been labouring for four days upon an article. The reader, perhaps, if any reader actually gets through it, will achieve the business in ten minutes, snickering idly the while over the transient jocosities, and maybe giving a belch or two of honest satisfaction, if he is intelligent, over the underlying ideational structure. A snicker, a grunt, a murmured "Not so bad." Is it enough? To earn that only half-articulate encomium I must suffer long-continued and intolerable agonies, sweating and groaning like a chorus girl in one of those Ziegfeld hip-shows that you admire. My heart must be wrung. My mind must be racked and torn. My diaphragm, stretched as tight as a drum-head, must give out a hollow, rumbling sound for days on end. The spectacle is almost revolting. Do you marvel that the average literatus, unsustained by my abnormal capacity for hearing psychic suffering, ends with his head a mush? There he sits in his austere room, striving hopelessly and abominably to dredge up ideas out of the black vast that they swim in, like half a dozen forlorn cockroaches in the illimitable reaches of the Pacific Ocean.

Nathan

You wring me. My collar chafes. My head swims. But you forget something, my dear doctor. The literatus suffers, but he is not actually alone. Nay, he has company in the death-house, and theologians on their way to hell. He has his conscience, as sharp as no razor ever was, and his memories, as sickly sweet as stale beer. He remembers the girl who wore the black and orange jersey. He remembers the girl who made him promise to stop drinking Aquavit. He remembers the girl who married the Congressman with the toupee and sent him back his faded valentines. He remembers what he owes, what he ate in 1902, what it felt like to be 30 years old, what he learned in college — all that he has endured in this damndest of all worlds. But this is only half of the story. After all, a man's conscience is usually so cowardly that it is afraid even of him, and so it doesn't bother him much — and his memories cloud and clot as the years go plunging by. But day in and day out his body is wasting, and as it wastes it hurts: the disintegration of colloids is painful. What man of forty can go into a room alone without feeling a dull ache somewhere? If it is not a twinge of lumbago, it is a sore tooth. If it is not a sore tooth, it is a gone feeling at the pit of the stomach. If the stomach is all right, it is a cough. If there is no cough, it is a tickling in the nose.

Mencken

Ah, the nose! What I have suffered! Twice broken, three times bulged and gashed by surgery, eight times bloodied in the wars and in fights with poets, women, booze-snouters, the rev. clergy. When I came into the world it had the symmetry of a Mycenaen amphora; to-day it is a brother to the artichoke.

Nathan

But here, of course, your suffering is chiefly psychical. It is the cosmetic chaos that you deplore; the actual algesia is very slight. But consider, more relevantly, the slow, ghastly process of renal disintegration. One by one the infundibular cells sicken and die — not a few dozen, or gross, or army corps, but billions and billions. Each yields up the ghost reluctantly. Each passes on to bliss eternal with all the frantic unwillingness of an archbishop. Each wages a desperate though fruitless battle with the pathogenic organisms, fatigue poisons, or alcohol. Imagine the effects on the man!

Mencken

The suggestion is apposite. Needless to say, it has occurred to me hitherto. When I go into my lonely writing chamber and sit down to compose I feel every twinge and alarm of every one of those kidney cells. The accumulated surgical shock is sometimes downright maddening. I break into a cold sweat. It is as if an infinite multitude of ultra-microscopic pins were being thrust through my gizzard. And in the room of every dead cell, once the carcass has been hauled away by the blood stream, there is scar-tissue — a stiff, unyielding, uncomfortable substance, as irritating as a speck of sand in the eye. As you hint, the effect on the literatus, penned up in his chamber with such tragedies, is almost maddening. It is only the dull brute, the stock broker or traffic cop turned author, who does not suffer. I am delighted that you don't dispute my doctrine.

Nathan

Dispute it? How could I dispute it? Do I jump when some one argues that two and two are four?

Mencken

(*Uncertainly*). Well, *do* you?

Nathan

The answer is yes and no. If *you*, for example, were to argue that two and two made four, then perhaps —

Mencken

But to return to our problem. The idea that you expose so neatly is, as I say, familiar to me. It has crossed my mind a thousand times when I was late with an article and trying to finish it on time. I have sat for four days trying to fetch up a single phrase — and had more pains and malaises in that time than a man with the botts. Literary endeavour is the cause of my hypochondria. I remember well one day when I was working on "A Book of Prefaces." So many aches suddenly appeared, North, East, South and West, that I jumped to the conclusion that I was coming down with lockjaw, with maybe Asiatic cholera as a complication. It was all I could do to keep from leaping to the window and yelling for the coroner. I suffered more in four hours than Debs has suffered in all his time at Atlanta.

Nathan

And no wonder! A Socialist is ideally fitted for going to jail. All his ideas are ready-made and quite solid, and so he can risk being alone. Socialism is thus a sort of insurance against insanity, like patriotism and religion. A man swallows it, gives up thinking, and is happy.

Mencken

What is called business has the same effect. It dulls the perceptions and so makes for happiness. As you know, I hate it quite as much as you do, but this hatred is largely snobbery: I am, to that extent at least, a genuine literary gent. As a matter of fact, I believe fully that our joint business affairs have been the salvation of both of us. Business engages the mind, but makes no actual demands upon it; it takes infinitely more concentrated mental effort to write even a bad fugue than it takes to start a national bank or swindle the government. A business man may thus suffer from mental decay for years, and never discover it. I could give you examples. But in the case of a literary man, the slightest departure from the normal shows itself at once: one concludes, reading his book, that the fellow is balmy. Hence free verse. Free verse is simply the pathological production of a poet who has gone crazy trying in vain to write poetry — a sort of toxin thrown off by a sprained mind. It has the same chemical and psychological basis as the inchoate words that religious maniacs babble at Methodist revivals.

Nathan

But enough of pathology! You are always talking of lesions, infections, blood counts, neuroses, comas, and such things. I am certainly no expert in etiquette, but it seems to me quite plain that it is bad taste to unload such graveyard stuff upon a man as old as I am. You have even infected *me*. Until I met you I had never heard of the staphylococci. Now I can feel a billion of them marching through my system to the tune of Mendelssohn's op. 103.

Mencken

I apologize if I have offended you. Nevertheless, it seems to me quite within the bounds of reason to argue that you owe your life to me. Six years ago, when you were in the hands of all those quacks, I scared you into consulting Dr. Barker, and Barker cured you. Otherwise, you might be dead by now.

Nathan

Yes, and at peace in hell. Why live on — with all those cocci gnawing into every sinew? I often wonder what you talk of to women. They all seem to like pathology. I suppose that when you get one behind the potted palms at the Plaza, the two of you have a session to make an undertaker faint.

Mencken

By no means. I always avoid the subject.

Nathan

Then what do you talk of?

Mencken

Literature. That is, unless the lady is literary herself. Then I praise her clothes.

Nathan

On what theory?

Mencken

It is not a theory; it is a matter of chivalry. For one of such gifts you show a very low power of psychological observation. Because the average literary woman, when she comes into a magazine office, looks like a fishmonger's wife dressed for the Inauguration Ball, you conclude idiotically that she rigs herself out in that fashion deliberately — that she makes herself a guy as a sort of defiance to her sex — a signal of her superiority. Nothing could be more untrue. The fact is that she invariably thinks her clothes are beautiful. Say that they are, and she is pleased.

Nathan

But why try to please her? I am an editor, not a modiste.

Mencken

As I have said, it is a matter of chivalry. I was born and brought up in the South, and I simply can't get rid of such ideas. Why do I denounce southern *Kultur* so often and so violently? Send a postcard to Professor Dr. Sigmund Freud, General Delivery, Vienna, and you will get the answer by return mail. Ask him to give my regards to Hermann Bahr.

Nathan

Now you are on psychoanalysis. Let up, in God's name! I almost prefer the lesions and streptococci.

Mencken

You shy at phantoms. When I think of psychoanalysis, as it is ordinarily understood, the effect upon me is precisely that of seeing a fat woman climbing to the roof of a Fifth Avenue bus. In brief, it fills me with obscene mirth. Dr. Freud is a diligent and well-meaning sheephead. He thinks he has demonstrated that all the ills and lunacies of the world are caused by suppressed sexuality. But all he has actually proved is that all the ills and lunacies of his readers are caused by suppressed sexuality. In other words, the only true Freudian cases are the Freudians.

Nathan

Yet you have often written sweet words of him.

Mencken

True — and I did it honestly. More, I'll probably do it again — also honestly. What I am telling you today is what I believe today, not what I believed last Tuesday, or what I shall believe come Michaelmas. My ideas change constantly. The truth, as I see it, is not made of concrete, but of gutta percha. It yields, moves, stretches, changes shape. The same truth is never true for the same man continuously. Let us assume that there is a certain of truths, numbered one, two, three, four, and so on, and a certain series of men, designated A, B, C, D and so on. Let us also assume that there is a series of adjacent days: Monday, Tuesday, Wednesday, etc. Now let us proceed to the hypothesis that Truth No. 1 is true for A on Monday, and that Truths No. 2, 3 and 4 are true for B, C and D on the same day. But is Truth No. 1 also true for A on Tuesday? Not necessarily. Not even probably. On Tuesday A believes in Truth No. 2. Meanwhile B has proceeded to Truth No. 3 and C to Truth No. 4. Now move on to Wednesday. What do you discover? That A has got to Truth No. 3, B has got to Truth No. 4 and so on down to X, who has got to Truth No. $n + xn$. So far, so good. Let us now assume that —

Nathan

I trust you will excuse me.

Mencken

I beg pardon?

Nathan

Your formula is instructive, but as you know, the exact sciences bore me. I have a special phobia against mathematics. Next to literature, it —

Mencken

You have my apologies.

Nathan

Say no more. What you endeavour to impart is, after all, quite clear to me. I do not reject the theory as untenable; I merely spit out the formula as offensive to me. As I take it, you mean to say that when a given truth survives it is no sign that anyone has cherished it over a given duration of time; it is simply a sign that believers in it have succeeded one another in an unbroken succession. This I grant you. It is the only truth of which a careful man may say without qualification that it is substantially true. What I believed in 1912 I no longer believe, but someone else *does* believe it — some pathetic ass. Thus every truth with any merit in it whatsoever is kept alive. As one crowd of believers goes out, another comes in.

Mencken

Very nobbily put. You grasp the idea magnificently. Today you preach a certain body of critical doctrines, the product of gazing nightly at herds of half-naked women in stuffy theaters. By tomorrow you will have begun to doubt these doctrines. But meanwhile they will be filched by the critics of the New York newspapers, translated into bad English, and launched upon the white-goods buyers who sit beside you in the show-houses. Next month or next year they will reach the critics of Pittsburgh and Kansas City; a year later they will conquer the Columbia faculty, and then the Yale faculty. But by that time you yourself will be quite purged of them, and so you will be made ill by the very thought of them. In their place you will have a new set.

Nathan

Profoundly true. But what of Tom Smith? He has believed continuously for twenty-two years that a pair of yellow spats make him look like the Right Hon. Arthur James Balfour. How do you account for that?

Mencken

Simply enough. Smith's belief in those spats is not logical, but merely emotional. It is a superstition, and hence transcendental; it has nothing whatever to do with the truth. I am speaking here of truths susceptible to evidential demonstration, not of hallucinations. Smith believes in spats precisely as a Maryland mouzhik believes in the madstone.

Nathan

Yet he is a sagacious fellow. His judgment of gin is infallible. Time and again I have tried to fool him with synthetic stuff. Every time he spouts it out, like a Chinaman sprinkling wash.

Mencken

That isn't sagacity; that is a reflex. The same thing causes you to blink your eye when a light suddenly flashes before you.

Nathan

Or when one of your lady poets comes into the office. The last one dam-nigh sent me headlong out of the window. I marvel that you can be so polite to them.

Mencken

Put down half of it to the chivalry aforesaid, and the other half to my interest in literature. The love of literature is, I suppose, in itself a form of chivalry: chivalry toward its creator's expressed or suppressed vanities. Give all literature your eye and you'll find that this is so, from Benvenuto Cellini, say, as one extreme, to Robert W. Chambers at the other. In each and every case, the written document is a polite, low bow to the writer — *as the writer desires to see himself.*

Nathan

If that theory is true, then what of such a writer as Harriet Beecher Stowe with her "Uncle Tom's Cabin?" Surely you don't argue that it was Harriet's secret desire to be a coon?

Mencken

Maybe not. But what the old gal *did* want to be was a bloodhound. She wanted in her stupendous vanity, to be a tracker-down, a scooter after fugitives, an instrument of vengeance, which is to say, justice. She was the lady Upton Sinclair of her day. Had she lived in 1907, she would have written Thomas W. Lawson's books. Had she lived in 1912, she would have written "My Little Sister" and the other white-slavery brochures. Had she lived in 1915, she would have written Cleveland Moffett's "Invasion of America." And were she alive today, she'd be bawling for the Blue Laws.

Nathan

Then, according to your theory, it is Maeterlinck's secret desire to be an unborn child. It is a pity that he got only the second half of his wish.

Mencken

That is mere prejudice. Maeterlinck is the archtype of the literatus, the perfect author, and hence you dislike him. Your error lies in confusing intelligence with æsthetic skill and passion. Have you ever met any musicians?

Nathan

Not since Prohibition.

Mencken

I mean creative musicians, not mere executants, however talented. Well, a few inquiries would convince you that a man may be a great composer, and yet quite balmy. Read Mozart's letters. Ponder the philosophizings of Beethoven. Think of the private career of Schubert.

Nathan

Alas, I know eleven music critics.

Mencken

Then I rest my case. There is but one music critic in America who was even *born* sane. All save this one are not simply balmy; they are actual morons. But what has sanity to do with art? Shakespeare was a sub-mastoid circular neurotic of the third declension, with hysterical overtones and plain evidences of pressure symptoms. Goethe had chronic interstitial dementia precox, complicated by oedema of the left lobe of the medulla oblongata. Molière was an hysteric of the third type, with acute agoraphobia. Dante had softening of —

Nathan

In other words, you contend that the balmier the bird, the better the artist. What of, say, D'Annunzio? If you are right, this Gabe should be the Shakespeare of the twentieth century.

Mencken

Gabe isn't balmy enough.

Nathan

Well then, what of Gorki?

Mencken

You are getting warm. But Maxie is balmy only in the second degree.

Nathan

Brieux?

Mencken

Warmer still. But —

Nathan

Tolstoi?

Mencken

You win!

————————

Conversation VI: "On Dress"

Scene: *The swimming-pool at the Biltmore.*
Time: *Ash Wednesday.*

Nathan

I note that you still wear B. V. D.'s. Isn't it a bit — well, say rather somewhat — ?

Mencken

Maybe sagacious is the word you seek.

Nathan

It is precisely the word I do *not* seek. What I get at is that a man of your years and dignity should clothe himself in a more seemly manner. I overlook your overcoats — or, rather, your overcoat. It symbolizes, perhaps, your defective relish for public applause. But a man's underwear symbolizes his view of himself. It constitutes an intimate and secret self-estimate. What he puts next to his epidermis reveals his private notion of his just deserts. Well, I am under no illusion that you regard yourself with anything approaching injustice. Therefore, I —

Mencken

Spare me your metaphysics! I wear B. V. D.'s for a plain reason. They are admirable, and they are cheap. Could you imagine garments more intelligently designed? Think of the old-style lingerie that we wore as boys — the thick, knitted undershirts, the long-legged sub-pantaloons. Did you ever hear of such a shirt that was comfortable, or of such a pantaloon that did not bunch at the ankles? Yet mankind suffered those abominations for years. Then, characteristically, American genius came to the rescue; it is constantly making the world more comfortable. It devised the B. V. D. — and at once wearing underclothes became a luxury. One never hears them discussed any more; they are as silent and efficient as a perfect head-waiter. In the old days every American man talked about his interior swathings. "Have you put on your heavy woolens

yet?" And so on. Now every intelligent American wears B. V. D.'s, and the subject has lost all point and interest.

Nathan

But you miss my contention. I don't object to the *design* of your inside wrappings. What astounds me is that a man so sniffish should wear such *materials*. If your chemise is not cambric, then it must be muslin, or calico, or something of the sort. And if you paid more than a dollar for it, then I license you to hold my head under water for ten minutes. Have you no respect for your person?

Mencken

Well, what should I wear, if not cotton? Wool? It scratches. Linen? It is clammy. Silk? It is bawdy. I don't like the feel of silk on my hide. It is far too caressing and luxurious. My work in the world is essentially serious. I am a sort of *liaison*-officer between the American intelligentsia and civilization. Could I do this work reposing on an oriental couch, smoking opium, and with a couple of loose girls dancing before me? Could I do it emersed in a tub of *pêche Melba?* Could I do it while the Boston Symphony Orchestra played "Geschichten aus dem Wiener Wald?" Naturally not. By the same token, I couldn't do it bundled up in silks and satins like one of Ziggy's poor working girls. The arts demand renunciation, simplicity, a touch of asceticism. The artist must know how to suffer.

Nathan

With all due regard for your feelings, mush! I can grant your whole case and still refute you. Wear a hair-shirt if you want to! Have your B. V. D.'s made of burlap. How does all this account for the hat you wear? Or for your habitual overcoat? Or for your 50-cent neckties? Beholding you loping along Fifth Avenue of an afternoon, one is reminded of a

Goldberg cartoon dramatized by Harry Kemp, with music by Erik Satie. It is my contention that such a hat as yours offers a subtle offense to all that is highest and finest in our Christian civilization.

Mencken

Nonsense. You exaggerate rhetorically. The hat is a genuine Knox and cost me a pretty penny. I have it cleaned once a year, and a new band put on. It is a dignified and seemly hat, and quite suitable to my station in life. As for the public effect, I am not interested in it. I suffer enough trying to instruct and elevate the public. It would be going too far to ask me to rejoice it æsthetically also. The hat is satisfactory to me and, I hope, to God. Let that suffice.

Nathan

Yet you allude to yourself as an artist.

Mencken

Exactly. But as an artist in ideas, not in haberdashery. I am not interested in clothes for the same reason that I am not interested in the postal regulations governing fourth-class matter, or the music of Vincent D'Indy, or the question of whether General Ulysses S. Grant went to heaven or to hell. Such matters do not appertain to my avocation, nor to my vices. I am not an actor, and so I don't work with my necktie. I am neither an Episcopal rector nor a stock-broker, and so it makes no difference whether my shoes are shined or not.

Nathan

Neither do you work with your front tooth. Yet, you employ a dentist to half sole and heel it annually, and if some woman threw a beer seidel at you and knocked it out you'd yell for the police.

Mencken

Naturally. I eat with my teeth, and eating is not only necessary to me, but a pleasure to me. In fact, it is probably my principal vice. No other vice has ever done me any harm, but I am even now in the hands of the faculty for eating too much. A genuinely tender and well turned Wiener schnitzel fascinates me almost as much as a Methodist deacon is fascinated by the *gluteus maximus* of a chorus girl. I'd gladly leave a hanging, or a performance of Beethoven's fourth — not his fifth or eighth! — or even a quiet chat with some cute one in the falling dusk for such a dinner as dear old Halévy used to serve in the last days of sound white wine. If, as you say, I dress like Jim Morgan in "Ten Nights in a Barroom," and look sartorially like a bad case of uticaria, then it is simply because clothes do not interest me. I do not aspire to be a Beau Brummel, any more than I aspire to be a vestryman of St. Bartholomew's. Fancy clothes or no fancy clothes, I am pretty enough. If I dressed up it would cause me trouble. I fear the Life Force.

Nathan

That you are a beautiful creature I do not gainsay. In all the zoos of the world there is not a rhinoceros more lovely. Nevertheless you must go clothed; you can't walk the earth in the altogether; it would be worse than Bolshevism. Well, being forced by law to garment yourself, why not do it with some good grace? That hat looks like an Allentown, Pa., cuspidor. It affects me like a woman without eyebrows. I don't argue that you should waste hours choosing neckties. All I contend is that you should not carry your disdain of sightly habiliments to the point of phrenitis.

Mencken

I return to my primary position. I am a trafficker in concepts and conjectures, not a dancing-master. I wouldn't write any better if my pantaloons were better creased. I don't criticize the world and its ideas with my shirt.

Nathan

But the world inevitably criticizes you *and* your shirt. You and your shirt would make a very tasty frontispiece for Sinclair Lewis' "Main Street," or George Ade's "Fables in Slang."

Mencken

And what of you? Does your greater application to the psychology of regalia get you anything? Say some fool gal is fetched by that new greenish suit of yours, and by that corn-flower boutonnière. What is the result? It costs you $15 or $20 to buy her a dinner, you both get a bad stomach-ache, and the next morning you come down to the office grumbling because she confided to you — during the five dollar dessert — that she was in love with a footballer at De Pauw University.

Nathan

As they put it in New Jersey, there is something into what you say. But what, in turn, does *your* indifference to costumerie get *you*? The only difference between us, so far as I can see, is that one look at you gives the gal stomachache without any dinner.

Mencken

What is that to me? My work in the world, as I have hinted, is not concerned with what gives people aches in the stomach, but with what gives them aches in the medulla oblongata. My concern is with epistemology, not with intestinal fermentation.

Nathan

Again you emit nonsense. What you say is simply the old "art for art's sake" buncombe in rather more disarming terms. Assuming that you are an artist, as you somewhat obstreperously maintain, then your duty as an artist is obviously to your art. But in addition there is your duty as a citizen. I contend that it is part of that duty to dress yourself in a respectable and tasteful manner, that there may be no unnecessary public scandal.

Mencken

My reply is that I already do so. Do you forget that E. W. Howe once pronounced me the best-dressed man in New York? Howe, true enough, has his defects as a critic of the fine arts. But in this department he was well within his jurisdiction, for he judged me *as an American citizen*. He himself is the archetype of the American citizen, and so I valued and still value his encomium. I question that you yourself have any right or capacity to estimate such things. You are no more American than absinthe, free speech or the sonata form. In the legend that you were born in Fort Wayne, Ind., I take no stock. That is, not permanently. Now and then, of course, I half believe it. When you bought that green necktie with orange spots I was pretty well convinced. But mainly I doubt it. More, everybody else doubts it. Whenever there is a war, the home-loving Vigilantes will accuse you of belonging to the enemy nation, whatever it is. But as for me, no one ever questions my patriotism: it is well known that all I suffer by living among Elks, Moose, Knights of Pythias, Odd Fellows and Maccabees is offered freely upon the altar of my country. Besides, there is the imprimatur of Howe, the most American of all Americans. He anoints me and hands me the cup. An apostolic succession. You can't gainsay it. Howe thought *you* were a Jap. He had been reading the California papers.

Nathan

Fair words, but I still mark your hat "Exhibit A" and hand it to the foreman of the jury.

Mencken

Whose name, I daresay, is Emil Krausmeyer. He will recognize the spatters of beer, and give me a *hoch*. As a patriot, I prefer the verdict of Howe.

Nathan

This Howe admires your façade because it is of the species *au fait* in his native Potato Hill. You are both neanderthal men sartorially. Sprinkle some baking soda on your hair, roll your *r's*, and I wouldn't be able to tell you from him. . . . You circle the point of argument. A civilized man's duty is to look like a civilized man, not like the window of a second-hand clothing store in the Jugo-Slovak quarter. When an eyesore like yourself moves down a street, he constitutes an affront to cosmic beauty. I sometimes think that you are in league with a syndicate of oculists.

Mencken

And thou? When a circus parade like yourself moves down the boulevard he constitutes an offense against everything but the high cost of living.

Nathan

You have little discernment; you are clothes-blind. I do not dress ostentatiously. On the contrary, my decorations are very *piano*. To a rube like you, any man whose collar is not three inches too large for him and whose cuffs are properly buttoned is a fop, and fit for the soft drinks. Anything beyond two ash-carts and an ice-wagon looks like a circus parade to a man in Pottstown.

Mencken

I repeat: my outward aspect is of no importance to me. I take no more interest in clothes than I take in bee-culture.

Nathan

Well, look at that fellow at the far end of the pool: a beer-keg with a face! Picture him walking down the street *in toto!* Go farther. Picture nine-tenths of the men and women you know walking down the street in the same state! Clothes keep a nation from laughing itself to death. You speak of the Life Force. The Life Force, four times out of five, is clothes, and little else. Shaw, who popularized the term in "Man and Superman," knew it, but was too timid to say so in so many words. Therefore, like Barrie, who is similarly a coward when it comes to stating openly and clearly anything that isn't already a platitude, he resorted to his customary stratagem of concealing it in the stage directions, where only "safe" persons might encounter it. He was afraid to trust himself with the idea before the mob. Turn to page 15 of the text of the play and to his description of Ann Whitefield, his Life Force instrument. He says: "Instead of making herself an eyesore, like her mother, she has devised a mourning costume of black and violet silk." Shaw's subsequent qualifications are only further evidences of his eternal timidity in the face of an idea that is not already generally accepted.

Mencken

I follow you only half way. In fact, you follow yourself only half way. You say the Life Force is clothes, and little else, and then you proceed to prove it by showing that some woman character in a Shaw play dresses herself up in order to vamp some anonymous idiot — an idiot who, when he appears before the actual audience, is seen to be an actor! My reply is that I have nothing to do with such piggery. Having no desire whatsoever to be retired to the stock-farm, I see no reason why I should engaud myself like an opera manager. My clothes cover my person. They are of sound material. Their colours are inconspicuous. All beyond that would be supererogation. Let us now leap into the pool and disport ourselves.

Nathan

One moment, and I am done. Clothes give biology its touch of poetry. Without clothes, human beings of any refinement would die of disgust. Clothes are the mirages which cause humanity to stagger upward and onward with a smile on its lips and hope in its heart. Where is life the happiest, the gayest? In the great capitals — Paris, London, New York — where men and women pay the most attention to their personal appearance. And where, on the contrary, is it the most sordid and dispiriting? In the yap towns and peasant centres where no one gives a damn what he or she looks like. Consider your own case honestly. Don't you feel something's wrong when you haven't shaved, or when your collar is soiled, or when there is a soup spot on your coat? It's not a matter of comfort, as you will doubtless presently maintain — a soiled collar is just as comfortable as a clean collar, and a spotted coat is just as comfortable as a spotless one — it's a matter of *looks*. Admit it, and let's dive in

Mencken

I admit nothing, save that, as your liver ossifies, you become an utter ijjit. What a notion, indeed — that in the little Methodist hells of the back country no one gives a damn what he or she looks like! Is it possible for the human mind to conceive a more thumping piece of tosh? The plain truth is, of course, that it is precisely in the hinterland that all questions of clothes are most important. In Paris, before the war — perhaps the most civilized town then visible in the world — a man could wear practically any imaginable clothes on the street, and go unnoticed. I myself, when ill with a fever there, once promenaded the Avenue de l'Opera wearing one black shoe and one yellow one, and with an American flag wrapped around my plug hat. Not a soul challenged me. But in such a place as Memphis, Tenn., the cops would have jailed me, and in the average small town in Iowa the peasants would have burned me as a witch. Interest in clothes does not run as civilization runs; it runs *inversely* as civilization runs. It is not in Paris, or Rome, or Munich, or the West End of London that people notice such things; it is in Paducah, Ky., Snow Hill, Md., and the Bronx. You are so horribly the cockney that you simply don't know anything about what goes on west of Union Hill, N. J. If you walked into the average grass town of Maryland wearing that fur overcoat of yours, with that ring on your finger, and with your smoke-coloured walking-suit, the mouzhiks would fall upon you and give you a severe beating.

Nathan

I take it, of course, that your own draperies do not affront them?

Mencken

They do not venture to have an opinion about my clothes. I was born and raised in those parts, and know how to keep the peasants in their places. But if I went into your native Fort Wayne, Ind., wearing my Russian fur hat or my ribbon of the *Ordre de la Chasteté*, third class, I'd fully expect to be taken to the watch-house by the town constable. If he let me remain at large; it would simply be because he mistook me for a circus press-agent or a New York dramatic critic. Or maybe a collector for the Armenians

Nathan

All this is hollow and without sense. You prove that civilized garments would cause popular uprisings in Maryland or Indiana, and you then argue therefrom that a civilized man should not wear them. This is what you are fond of terming pish-posh. I array myself in a quiet manner, but do not disdain the elegances appropriate to the season, my surroundings and my station in life.

Mencken

I refuse to let you say anything so destructive to your dignity. Say that you were that fur coat because you like, now and then, a gaudy touch — because you frankly enjoy dressing up a bit — and I'll overlook your weakness. I have worse myself. Why do I part my hair in the middle

— a fashion that went out thirty years ago? So far as I know, only two other men in the civilized world still do it: Frank Harris and Fürst von Bülow. Well, why do *I* do it? Simply because it is a petty vanity. I confess it freely, and invite all critics of it to go to hell. But when you say that wearing a fur overcoat in New York is appropriate to your station in life, then I protest against the libel. Last night, on my way to the theater with you, I encountered exactly seven other men in such coats. One was a one-night-stand tragedian, one was a writer of popular songs, one was a curb-broker, one was a press-agent, one was a viola player in the Philharmonic Orchestra, one was the music critic of the *Daily Underwear News*, and the other I didn't know. I don't mention the chauffeurs.

Nathan

Let your point go into the minutes. But your whole logical method is fatal to your case. I saw only three hats like yours between the Beaux Arts and the Century Theater. One was on the head of a pickpocket who had just been taken *in flagrante delicto* by the cops, one was worn by a blind man at Broadway and 47th street, and one was lying in the gutter at 51st street. I should be delighted to have your interpretation of these facts.

Mencken

I do not attempt to interpret them. They have, in fact, no significance whatsoever. My hat means nothing; it is a mere blob. One either notices it or doesn't notice it. But a fur overcoat challenges the attention. It is deliberately *worn* to challenge the attention. My point is that the attention thus evoked is humiliating to a man of your dignity. The worst anyone could conceivably suspect me of being, looking at my hat, is an apartment house janitor or a professor at Columbia University. But looking at your coat, an otherwise quite intelligent person might reasonably mistake you for, say, a vaudeville headliner, the conductor of a German *Liedertafel*, or a member of the Union League Club. I leave the case to posterity.

Nathan

Well, then, if you are so disdainful of mere investiture, why not simply dress your soul, and let your carcass go bald? I offer to stand on the steps of the Public Library — near the left lion — and watch you pass. You will learn soon enough the politico-socio-economic importance of clothes. There are five gendarmes at Fifth avenue and 42nd street. I offer ten to one that even the fattest of them reaches you and lands his club upon your coco before you escape down the sewer.

Mencken

I begin to despair of you. Now you try to argue that clothes are important by showing that policemen think they are important. What next? A policeman is a man who is fined $2 if he reports for work without his shoes shined. *Ergo*, he believes that having his shoes shined is more important than —

Nathan

But what of Ibsen? He had his shoes shined twice a day.

Mencken

Ibsen? Now you introduce Ibsen! God help us all! Tell the coroner that I leave my sapphires to Eleanor. Give Marie my —

(*He dives.*)

Nathan

Your hat?

(*He dives.*)

———————————

Conversation VII: "On Editing a Magazine"

Scene: *Campbell's Funeral Church.*

Time: *Between two funerals.*

Mencken

The scene just brought to a harmonious close has greatly depressed me. What could be more pathetic than the funeral of a magazine editor?

Nathan

Perhaps the funeral of a magazine.

Mencken

I doubt it. So far, I have never attended one — if, in fact, they are ever held — but I once went to the funeral of a newspaper. I was the chief mourner. Nay, I was a sort of right hind leg of the actual corpse. Nevertheless, the whole thing was banal — as flabby and disappointing as a beheading or a honeymoon. All the great overt acts of life are similarly pifflish. One thinks of dying as of a great adventure. It is, in reality, simply a colossal exaggeration of having a tooth pulled. Maybe not that. Even in war a man seldom faces death in the full possession of his faculties. He is usually in a stupour; if he is not in a stupour he is scared so badly that he is almost anæsthetic. Thus he dies, so to speak, boozy. It is no worse, I daresay, than kissing a woman congressman when one is drunk.

Nathan

But if my recollection serves me you were but recently saying that the funeral of a magazine editor is pathetic.

Mencken

His funeral, yes — but not his death. The funeral is not a natural process; it is a work of art — the fruit of thousands of years of idealistic ingenuity among millions of asses. Need I remind you that a work of art is always more poignant and moving than anything produced by unaided nature? Compare the average woman in the altogether with the same woman in her best frock, or even in a *robe de nuit*. Only Puritans believe that the human body, the masterpiece of the Creator, is beautiful in itself; only Puritans are moved by it. Some, moved only so far, become bad artists and try to paint it. Others, moved intolerably, bawl for the gendarmes. Both factions are swine.

Nathan

I hope you will not be affronted if I tell you that it is my natural tendency to suspect your ideas. But in this case you appeal to my judgment. Unquestionably, a gal dressed up tastily is more appetizing to the eye than the same mammal in toto. More, it is still pleasanter merely to dream about her than actually to meet her, even dolled up. I have a theory that no intelligent man ever loves a woman truly until he knows her so well that he doesn't really see her when he talks to her — that is, until she ceases to arrest his actual attention. What he talks to thereafter is an artificiality created by his own imagination. If the woman is clever she quickly converts herself into this artificiality, or, at all events, tries to do so. If she succeeds, the man is lost. His ideal has him by the ear.

Mencken

You rise to my notion very gracefully. Thus I assume that I have your support in the matter of funerals. Death itself is a mere chemical reaction, and no more interesting, at bottom, than the fermentation that goes on in a vat of beer. But the ensuing funeral is romantic, appealing, almost voluptuous. It is to the mere physical blow-off what a superb drinking song, say "Toss the Pot" or the *brindisi* in "Giroflé-Giroflá" is to the lowly offices of Emil, the brewery sexton. Poetry goes into a funeral. It may be the poor, pitiful poetry of stupid and unimaginative persons, but it is poetry none the less. A dog dies like a man, but a dog could not imagine a funeral. Even an Odd Fellows' funeral would be beyond him. Have you ever been to an Elks' lodge of sorrow? No? Then go the next time Frank Crowninshield invites you. They have a large bank of electric lights on the stage, and as the names of the brethren laid away during the year are read by the Supreme Worthy Lugubrious the lights go out one by one. He reads "Hermann Metwurst," and out goes a light. Then "Terence Casey," and out goes another, Then "Gerald Hornstein," and out goes a third. And soon. Don't laugh! It is, superficially, idiotic, just as it is superficially idiotic for a man to come out on a public stage and begin hauling a hank of horsehair over the embalmed duodenum of a cat. But under the surface indecency, in each case, there is a noble striving toward beauty. The Elks are poets. They try to make death lovely and pathetic.

Nathan

I catch your point. You argue that the funeral of a magazine editor is pathetic, but concede that the pathos is intrinsic in the funeral, and not derived from any nobility or dignity in the life and career of the man himself. The concept is certainly not obnoxious to me. But if you had argued that —

Mencken

Oh, by no means!

Nathan

In any case, the dead editor himself is of small interest. He is even of less interest dead than he was alive. Have you ever heard of anyone — that is, any stranger, say a distinguished French or British visitor — going out to a graveyard to put a tin wreath on the grave of a magazine editor? Who knows, indeed, where the editor of *Godey's Lady's Book* is buried? To achieve an almost perfect obscurity a magazine editor doesn't even have to die; all he has to do is to lose his job. Consider, for example, Edward W. Bok. Twenty years ago, in the full flush of his editorial glory, he was one of the most eminent men in the country. Today he is scarcely more heard of than Johann Sebastian Bach.

Mencken

Melancholy fancies, to be sure! Yet there is an undoubted allurement in the profession. All authors wish that they were editors. Even you and I, who are certainly devoid of most of the ambitions which harass literary gents, are nevertheless quite willing to do the most menial tasks for *The Smart Set* — for instance, translating American short stories into English, punctuating poetry, and going out to dinner with novelists, playwrights and publishers.

Nathan

And why not? The editorial chair is a vampire for two plain reasons. In the first place, editing a magazine is one of the easiest jobs known in Christendom. Anyone, in fact, is able to fill it — that is, any literate man. He may be unable, of course, to fill it successfully, but all the same he can fill it. This is certainly not true of most other human vocations. To cut off a leg, however badly, a man must at least have a modest grounding in the elements of anatomy and pathology. To defend a criminal in the courts, he must at least know the common jargon of the law, and be able to distinguish between the judge on the bench and the chief perjurer for the People. To preach the word of God, he must at least be apparently sober and have on his pantaloons. But a magazine editor is required to show no such fundamental competence. If he can read and write, that is enough. All the rest is mere *lagniappe*. I have edited *The Smart Set* when suffering from such severe neuralgia that I could not distinguish between a pretty miss and a major-general in the Army at ten paces. I have done it when full of so vile a megrim that the roof of my head seemed to lift six inches every time I drew breath. I have done it after receiving such a letter from a fair creature that many a man would have leaped forthwith out of the sixteenth story window. No doubt you yourself have even stranger tales to tell. Now and then you send me word from Baltimore that some one down there has pulled off a beer-party surpassing anything ever heard of by the Romans. For two or three days thereafter I get no direct word from you; you are apparently quite unable to write a simple picture-postcard. Nevertheless, you continue your editorial functions all the while, and show all of your normal competence. So far as I can remember, you have never delayed reading or punctuating a manuscript for any such reason. You may be laid up at the Johns Hopkins, with two or three nurses laving you with ammonia, but all the same you remain as good an editor as you ever are.

Mencken

I fear you exaggerate my disability. I never —

Nathan

Exactly. But certainly you will admit that there are times when, for this or that physical or psychical reason, you are quite unable to compose a single line of passable prose. And certainly you will also admit that you are quite competent, at such times, to perform your editorial duties — that is, as well as you ever perform them.

Mencken

On reflection I am disposed to agree with you, at least tentatively. But what is the second lure you mentioned?

Nathan

The lure of being able to print one's own compositions *ad lib*. This, I take it, is what fetches the great majority of literati. There never lived an author without a grievance of some sort or other against an editor. It is a universal pestilence. And out of the grievance grows the notion of a remedy. That remedy is to set up shop as an editor one's self. Very few authors, of course, ever find it possible to do so. Hence they hate the small number of authors who do. *Ergo*, the auctorial hatred of editors is doubly-distilled.

Mencken

And absolutely justified. As you have already demonstrated, a magazine editor is probably the most incompetent professional man in the world; he is even more incompetent than the theologian who swindles poor old women by promising to save them from hell. The theologian at least does his damndest; not infrequently he actually believes in his own preposterous sorceries. But the magazine editor is simply a scoundrel. In his dealings with authors he is utterly without conscience.

Their livelihood, their peace of mind, their very sacred honour is and are in his hands. Yet who ever heard of him paying any heed to such things? His one aim is to sell his puerile and scabrous magazine. If he can do it by debauching and degrading an author, he never hesitates an instant. The beaches of beautiful letters are covered with the carcasses of his victims. I scarcely know of an author who has not been brought down in the world of the spirit by his dealings with magazines. Their influence is almost invariably corrupting. No man can pass through the magazines without gross damage to his spiritual kidneys. For this the editor is to blame.

Nathan

As an author, I agree with you. But as a magazine editor, I file a caveat. You are altogether too damned sweeping. In witness whereof I point to myself as Exhibit A. Show me an author that I have thus brought down.

Mencken

The answer is two-fold. On the one hand, you are surely a hell of an editor, judged by any intelligible standards, On the other hand —

Nathan

I dispute it. On the contrary, it seems to me that I am almost the ideal editor — that is, from the standpoint of an author. And for a simple reason. I never give a hoot about the public taste; for all I care, the public may rot away in its wallow. All I ask is that the author send in something that pleases *me*. If he does, then I vote for it. This, of course, bars out whole categories of authors. Nothing that Ellen Key, say, could write, or Dr. Frank Crane, or Herbert Adams Gibbons, or Blasco Ibáñez, or Isaac Marcosson, or Corra Harris, could ever conceivably caress my gills. But I am surely not unjust to such authors. I simply deny them justice altogether, and notify them of it in advance. They are wholly devoid of standing in my editorial court, just as a man who believes in the Constitution is in the Supreme Court of the United States. Let them beware! In point of fact, they accept the situation without complaint. So far as I am aware Blasco has never uttered a word against me, though he was long ago notified that I regard him as a clown. But to all other authors I am almost ideally hospitable. All they have to do is to send in something that happens to tickle me — and then you — and the cheque goes out on Thursday.

Mencken

A simple and honest system, but it has its drawbacks nevertheless. Suppose you happen to be bilious? What then?

Nathan

The bitter goes with the sweet. True enough, there are days when I am full of acids, and nothing seems good to me. But on the other hand there are days when I feel like a girl at her first party, and then I am surely an easy mark.

Mencken

It is on such days that I earn my honorarium. If the stuff that you vote for actually got into the magazine, then the barber shops would begin to take it in as a comic paper.

Nathan

Maybe so. But the fact that you exist is part of my theory. It takes two editors to play this novel and delicate game. On the days when I am too happy, and hence too easy, you are usually suffering from arterio-sclerosis, or lumbago, or tonsilitis, or one of your other curses, and so you act as a fly-wheel. And *vice versa*. Many a time, within a day or two after some elderly wench has smiled at you, you have passed to me manuscripts so bad that their publication would have ruined both of us. Fortunately, every such occasion has found me suffering with a ringing in the ears or spots before the eyes, and so I have saved the magazine.

Mencken

As you say, and *vice versa*. But all the same, the system has its defects — that is, from the standpoint of the author. It is easier for him, true enough, to please the two of us than it is for him to meet the notions of some poor outcast who is trying his darndest, by some theory of least squares, to work out what the people want out in Akron, O., or Sheboygan, Wis. You and I are at least concrete men, and moderately sane. The average magazine editor is simply a preposterous formula, and against all sense. But none the less, the author is hampered by our prejudices. He must compose something that lies without the range of our tastes.

Nathan

Well, it is *our* magazine, not his. Moreover, he has one plain advantage: he is trying to please a pair of literary birds, who at all events have the prejudices that are common to the trade, and that he himself may be presumed to share. Very few other magazine editors in America are literary birds themselves. Go over the list. There is ——, for example. How often hasn't he told us that he was apprenticed to a gambler in his youth, and that he wishes heartily that he were a faro-dealer today? Then there is ——, by trade a college professor. Then there is ——, an ex-clergyman, unfrocked for a very secular transaction with a fat contralto. Then there is ——, a newspaper reporter. What was —— four years ago? Press-agent for a celebrated courtesan. What was ——? A carpet-sweeper salesman. What was ——? A lawyer. What was ——? An osteopath.

Mencken

Your remarks, in general, are very instructive, and even convincing. It is obviously advantageous to an author to deal with editors who are also authors. But I often wonder if, in the long run, it is an advantage to an author to *be* an editor. Take my own case. At least four times a month I receive intolerably bad manuscripts from the literary critics of obscure provincial papers — and sometimes from critics who are anything but obscure. Well, whenever I send one back, accompanied by a polite rejection slip, I am subsequently denounced in the Oil City *Bugle* or the St. Joseph *Staats-Zeitung* as an idiot and a scoundrel.

Nathan

Well?

Mencken

I don't object to the conclusion; I object to the reasoning.

Nathan

Pish! What is the difference? Suppose the Oil City *Bugle*, instead of calling the attention of the Department of Justice to you, *praised* you? Then what? Some woman's club in the town would invite you to lecture, and the local Baptist university would propose to make you an LL.D.

Mencken

Nonsense. That is exactly what happens now. Your understanding of women, as I have often argued, is very defective. Every time I am denounced in some provincial newspaper as an immoral author, the women's clubs for miles around invite me to lecture. You assume that women admire the poor fish they marry. Far from it. They may respect such vermin in a way, but they don't like to hear them talk. When they get together for a pleasant afternoon they want to hear racy stuff. Well, they know what is in all the books praised by their local papers — optimism, idealism, patriotism, encouragement to noble living. *Ergo*, they read the books most violently denounced. *Encore ergo*, they want to hear the authors. This brings down a nuisance upon my head. I have to write lying letters of declination, saying that I am down with sciatica or on my honeymoon.

Nathan

Is it, then, unpleasant to lie to women? What a philosophy!

Mencken

Monotony is never pleasant. Nor is it agreeable to get money by false pretenses. Whenever I send a rejection slip to a provincial critic, I am sure of a round slating, and every time I get a round slating my books sell in that town, and my royalties increase. Well, the trouble is that the women who buy my books under such circumstances are swindled. They expect very hot stuff; what they get is metaphysics. Worse, their sense of having been defrauded converts itself, by a well-known psychological process, into the notion that *I* have defrauded them. As a matter of fact, I have done nothing of the sort. All I have done has been to perform a routine act of editorial vigilance.

Nathan

Well, my case is worse. You send back forty times as many manuscripts as I do — and yet I am attacked in exactly the same way. What is to be done about it?

Mencken

Nothing. I have a complete record of all such transactions running back five years. I even have sworn copies of many of the manuscripts submitted. I have often thought of printing the whole thing in a book, to be called, say, "*The Smart Set* Rejection-Slip Association" — first, the bad manuscripts; then the ensuing slatings. But it would be too cruel. Moreover, it would be silly. Any man who writes a book is an ass. He deserves all the punishment that he gets.

Nathan

Still, you lament rather ineptly. Think — as I have said — what would happen to us if those fellows praised us; indeed, think what actually did happen — in the case of "The American Credo." There we sat ourselves down and composed a tome that studiously insulted every American institution and every Americano that we didn't like and, lo and behold, the whole caboodle of newspaper reviewers hopped on the beer-keg and agreed with us absolutely. With what result, my friend? The book was a flat failure. Knopf had to sell his wolf-hound and his collection of lemon-yellow neckties to pay his rent that month. Once let the newspaper sodality begin to like our brand of hokum, and we're done for. Before "The American Credo," our books, subjected to constant and vicious drum-fire, were successes. With the "Credo" came good notices, and the threat of ruin. I have a feeling that the newspaper boys and girls, seized with a sudden astuteness, did the thing deliberately.

Mencken

That is always the way it happens. Plant your gun carefully, load it with a well-polished shell, blaze away at what seems to be the psychological instant — and you miss the mud-turtle by a mile. The intrinsic trouble was that the book was printed a year too late. Had we rushed it into type when we first thought of it, it would have made a smash.

Nearly all patriotic booksellers would have refused to handle it, it would have been barred from the mails, and Knopf would have been jailed. But we wasted so much time putting it together that when it came out at last it fell flat. In the interval a quite simple thing happened: the country reacted violently against the Wilsonian blather. On all sides the national superstitions began to be questioned. As a result the book was an anti-climax. We simply underestimated the force and speed of the reaction against Wilson and his balderdash. The man was so dead when our book came out that even the boobs in the street sniffed as they passed him. But something may yet be done. Such publications as Upton Sinclair's pamphlet, "The Brass Check," offer me a chance to write and print a violent attack upon the newspapers. This may prick some tender hides, and so get us some hearty slatings. At all events, it will be worth trying. At bottom, however, I fear that it is too late. Even the most tremendous attacks, considering the general state of public opinion, could scarcely ever again put the book on its feet. A newspaper review is not a fire, it is simply a match. If the boobs are ready, it sets them off. If they are not, they don't notice it.

Nathan

Let us bury the corpse, and forget it. Mons. Knopf makes altogether too much money out of us as it is. What interests me more at the moment is a delicately polite scheme for getting rid of the newspaper book reviewers who come to call on us in person with their manuscripts, and get sore when we send out word that we can't see them as we are receiving only blondes under twenty-two and bootleggers that day.

Mencken

I have long had my mind on the same subject. I have an idea or two to suggest when you are done. What is your plan?

Nathan

I suggest that we let the boys and girls in.

Mencken

Never! How could we get rid of them once they *were* in? They sit like so many mustard plasters.

Nathan

Comes now my idea. I have evolved a sweet device. Let us have a hole of some three inches in diameter bored through the partition into the adjoining office. Behind this hole, situated near the floor, let us station Marcel, the office lad. To this Marcel let us vouchsafe such a smoke-making apparatus as they use on the theatrical stage. Upon a pre-arranged signal, say a prodigious nose-blow on your part, let the afore-said Marcel apply the smoke machine to the hole and forthwith burst into the office crying out that the dump is on fire. There you have it!

Mencken

A nobby stratagem, I grant you. But it has one defect. The reviewer would already be so suffocated by the brand of cigar you smoke that he wouldn't notice our Marcel's efforts. I have a better plan. Let us eliminate our Marcel and merely hand our guest one of the cigars.

Nathan

I have tried it. It doesn't work. The last three visitors smacked their lips and stuck to their chairs.

Mencken

Yet these things, after all, are not our most serious problems. True enough, when it comes to problems we are much better off than nine-tenths of the other magazine editors, since we needn't give a damn one way or the other. If what we give our readers pleases them, good. If what we give them doesn't please them, also good. They get too much for their thirty-five cents as it is. We don't charge them enough. We can, without interference on the part of some Munsey or other, stick to our policy of printing nothing that we are not both sure of — that is, if we can get enough stuff of that sort. Questions of "advisability" and the like — the bane of the average editor — need never concern us. More magazines have been wrecked by this search for advisability than anything else I can think of, save it be too much money.

Nathan

I am in full accord with you. Consider two of the greatest magazine successes of recent years in America: the *Saturday Evening Post* and the

Atlantic Monthly, a brace of corpses revived into tremendous vigour. Well, neither Lorimer of the *Post* nor Sedgwick of the *Atlantic* bothers specifically about what it is advisable to print, nor even about what his public wants. Each simply prints what he likes himself. Both have made fortunes for themselves and the entrepreneurs behind them by assuming that what they like will also be liked by thousands of other right-thinking men. Our opportunity is just as clear. Let us assume that there are thousands of other Americans who have just as little virtue in them as I have, and just as little taste as you.

Mencken

What you say diverts and instructs me. You have reached such a stage of cunning that you can put my own ideas into such ingratiating phrases that they convince even me. Magazine editing at its most proficient is simply a tournament in autobiography. The more an editor tries deliberately to please the public, the quicker he comes a cropper. If he pleases himself — as, say, Siddall of the *American* pleases himself — he gets rich, and wears diamonds. Look over the list of magazine editors and publishers who have tried to please not themselves, but the public: McClure, Walker, John Phillips, Ridgeway, Munsey, Collier — there's no need to lengthen the catalogue. One and all, blooie!

Nathan

They are bringing in the next coffin. Let us depart.

Mencken

Where's my hat?

Nathan

Which hat was it?

Mencken

The one I bought six years ago and always wear.

Nathan

Doubtless in the coffin.

(Exeunt)

————————————

Conversation VIII: "On Marriage"

Scene: *A dormitory at Muldoon's Health Farm.*
Time: *5 A. M.*

Nathan

(*Rolling out of his cot.*) Come on; it's time to get up. In a minute that damned Irishman will be here with his cold squirt-hose.

(*No answer*).

Nathan

(*Beating on the washstand with his shoe.*) Arise, colleague, and to the day's torture!

(*Suddenly Mencken sits up in his cot, stares about him wildly, and then leaps to the middle of the floor.*)

Mencken

Name of a name! What a hell of a dream! It must be that sour clabber they gave us last night.

Nathan

What did you dream?

Mencken

I dreamt that I was married!

Nathan

You must be going crazy. Such dreams are pathological. Did you notice what the victim looked like?

Mencken

(*With early morning irascibility.*) Victim? She seemed well enough pleased with herself. You could see her wedding ring a block. It looked as thick as an automobile tire.

Nathan

Let us buy a dream-book when we get back to New York, and find out what such a dream signifies.

Mencken

No need. I am a Marylander, and every Marylander knows all the dream books by heart. They never do anything down there without consulting them. Dreams are never obvious. That is, one can't interpret them literally. Now take this dream that just awoke me, with cold sweat pouring down my face. What does it amount to, put into plain words? Simply to this proposition: "I fear that I am married." Well, both elements have to be interpreted — the "I" part and the "fear that I am married" part. Neither, as I say, is to be taken literally. Now, then, let us substitute. In place of "I," I put "you"; in place of "fear that I am married," I put its opposite, "ought to be married." *Ergo*, we arrive at the interpretation of the dream: you ought to be safely and respectably married.

Nathan

A superb tid-bit of ratiocination, and eminently characteristic of your logical processes! What actually awakened you with cold sweat pouring down your nose was not the dream but, obviously, the interpretation of it. The idea of my being safely and respectably married aroused your subconscious sympathy for me to such a degree that it woke you up in order that you might consciously satisfy yourself it wasn't true. Such nonsensical talk of matrimony is offensive to me.

Mencken

Naturally. It is also offensive to you when the Irishman rubs you down with that stable-broom. What is good for you is never pleasant. Did you enjoy castor oil when you were a boy? Or logarithms at college? Do you chuckle and snicker when you pay your tailor? Indubitably no. Well, I don't argue that marriage would delight you, say as a fine bottle of Scharlachberger 1910 delights you, or maybe a carafe of Saint-Estèphe or a sniff of Ploussard. What I argue is that it would be salubrious for you, advantageous to you, beneficial to your spirit. It would mellow and civilize you.

Nathan

I am already too highly civilized. Were it not for the overdose of civilization that has been inculcated in me, I should doubtless have been married long ago. That marriage civilizes a man, I do not gainsay. But to ask a man already civilized to get civilized all over again is like asking him to wear two undershirts. Furthermore, I dispute that marriage would benefit my spirit. It would make me too happy, and I couldn't do my work if I were too happy. A persistent touch of melancholy is essential to artistic enterprise. A happy man may be a successful bishop, dog-catcher, movie actor or sausage-monger, but no happy man ever produced a single first-rate piece of painting, sculpture, music or literature. I have aspirations.

Mencken

Dispute it all you please: the fact remains. The life you lead is too lonely. It throws you in upon yourself too much. Hence your hallucinations. Two or three weeks in that padded celibate cell of yours and I'd be seeing things too. Ghosts would hide in the waste-basket and jump out of the spittoon. What you need is a counter-irritant — a devoted wife to watch over you and police you, with maybe half a dozen little ones to break your rest and keep you constantly alarmed. A siege of measles would be a good thing for you. It would take your mind off your own malaises. I am a great believer in marriage. It is a noble institution. It keeps a man in health and order. It surrounds him with threats and menaces. It makes a better citizen of him. If you were married you wouldn't have to come to this Golgotha to be currycombed and manhandled by Muldoon's bouncers.

Nathan

But where would I find the devoted wife that you so touchingly describe? It is inconceivable that any woman, once she penetrated my many superficial charms, could be devoted to me. Never was there such an ignoble crank! If, after ten mellifluous years of marriage and after giving birth to our fourteenth beautiful child, my loving wife were one day to so much as snitch a favourite lead-pencil off my writing table, I would probably proceed forthwith to the big scene from "The Chinatown Trunk Mystery." I am not designed for marriage any more than a longshoreman is designed for Christian Science. But, after all, what has marriage to do with virtue? This place is full of married men. They drink just as much as I do, and sit up just as late Saturday nights.

Mencken

Then they are married unhappily. But you would be happy. Despite your gabble about your temperament, you have all the necessary talents. You are not cranky, but very polite. You notice what women have on, and praise it convincingly. You can stand their conversation. You like children. I advise you to marry the first respectable white woman who applies, and settle down with her decently.

Nathan

You talk like the Woman's Page in *Comfort*. To hear you rant, one would think that you yourself had a wife, and ten children. Or maybe even two wives.

Mencken

It is my loss that I haven't — and the world's. I venerate the institution.

Nathan

Then why are you still a bachelor?

Mencken

What a question! Why should I marry, who have no gift for it? I dislike women and hate children. Your logic is full of holes. Is it necessary for a man who admires baseball, for example, to play baseball? It is not. I elect to view marriage from a seat in the cosmic bleachers. I am a fan, not a performer.

Nathan

But how you can still admire the institution after giving so much powerful study to it is more than I can grasp. I know intimately some thirty sensitive, civilized married men and women, and not one of them

THE SMART SET CONVERSATIONS

but would go back to the solo life instanter if he or she could do it. Marriage may not be a failure, as the platitude goes, but it is surely a fire sale. A married man is one who has been badly damaged by the already burned-out fire of his love. The same with a married woman.

Mencken

I hold against you. Marriage is an insurance against romance. It makes a man safe, and secure, and comfortable. Did you ever know a bachelor who was in as good health as the average benedick?

Nathan

No. But that proves nothing. I never knew a bachelor who was in as good health as the average mule.

Mencken

You overlook the protection that marriage affords a man. Married, he is safe from nine-tenths of the hazards that continually confront the man who isn't married. Surely you will not deny that the unpleasant features of wedlock are compensated for by its single virtue of placing a man in the position of having no longer to maneuver elaborately day in and day out to escape marriage. Think of the relief, the peace of mind, the charm of such a position!

Nathan

According to your philosophy, it would be an equal relief for a one-legged man to have his other leg cut off, thus freeing his mind from the question of legs altogether.

Mencken

Not at all. A man with legs never thinks about them. But cut them off, and legs become the subject constantly uppermost in his mind.

Nathan

We are not discussing musical comedy, my friend, but marriage. And you have not yet advanced a single argument that soundly supports your regard for it. You say that marriage keeps a man in good health. Well, so do heavy doses of cod-liver oil and flannel belly-bands. You say that it safeguards his mind for all time from further thought of marriage. Well, so does locomotor ataxia. Your cures are worse, and even more bitter, than the diseases.

Mencken

You argue in circles — nay, in zigzags. For one thing, you assume fatuously that I regard a love affair as a secure basis for marriage. Nothing could be more absurd. Love is a casual matter, a chance infection, a thing not unlike a cold in the head. The process of falling in love is as fortuitous and trivial as the process of missing a train. Some fair one, hearing that one has recently received an LL.D. from Yale or made a killing at some swindle, goes to a beauty parlour, has her eyebrows gummed, puts on her best frock, and then leers at one across a dinner-table. The result, by a well-known psychological route, is the genesis of the idea that she has lovely eyes and a beautiful character, and that it would be charming to give her a hug. Or maybe the thing is pure accident. Perhaps she goes to the party without the slightest thought of serious professional business — and one is floored by the perfume she happens to wear, or by her anecdote of her little nephew, Lafcadio, or by the pretty way she takes it when the Colonel upsets his *potage Arlesienne* down her leg, or by the peculiar manner in which her hair is banged, or by the striking combination of cerise and non-cerise in her fourth-best party dress. Such is love, a madness worse than hydrophobia. To say that a man should be in love when he marries is to say that a ship-captain should be doubled up with cramps when he steers down the Ambrose Channel. It is a folly.

Nathan

Although I am not the authority on love that you appear to be, I permit myself to disagree with you. If falling in love is as easy as you say, set me down at once as *non compos womentis*. No less than one thousand times in my life have I assiduously tried to fall in love, but to be baffled. All the time that I have been eloquently trying to convince myself that the gal eating dinner at my expense was a divine mélange of Saint Saëns, apricots and chiffon, some irrepressible hanswurst within me has confounded me with the hypothesis that she was merely another

Lucile gown that hadn't had enough lunch. My imagination and my intelligence meet, to my sorrow, at an eternal Château Thierry. I have thus far fallen in love, during the thirty-nine years of my life, with twenty-seven lace and linen baby collars, eighteen bobbed hairs, forty-three blue dresses, ten lisps, thirty-six pairs of hands on my forehead when I was down with neuralgia, and eleven dozen initialed handkerchiefs and laundry bags, but not with a single girl. What, therefore, am I to do about it? I am helpless. And to ask me to marry a girl I don't love is to ask me to go to Buffalo when I have business in Chattanooga.

Mencken

The love you describe is quite enough. Love is not a goal, but a starting point. Your very incapacity for love suits you ideally for marriage. Just as the greatest heroic feats in war are performed not by experienced soldiers but by novices, so would the marriage of an amateur like yourself turn out a magnificent thing.

Nathan

Pursuing the same logic, I suppose that you argue that the man afflicted with arteriosclerosis makes the best ballet dancer.

Mencken

Not at all. What I contend is that your admiration for a few dollars' worth of lace around a gal's neck is of just as great horse-power as some other fellow's admiration for the gal *in toto*. Many a man has married for love no better supported, and has been happy. The great lovers of history haven't fallen for women, but for teeth, hair, eyes, smiles, silk garters, or a "No," as the case may have been.

Nathan

You comfort me, but you fail to convince me. Say I am floored, as I was at 5:30 P. M., standard Eastern time, last Wednesday, by a remarkable set of teeth. Say I were to lift those teeth into a taxi-cab, shoot to the Little Church Around the Corner, and swear to love, honour and obey them for the rest of my natural life. Explain to me now how thirty-two pretty teeth would operate to keep me in order, improve my health, make a better citizen of me, and safeguard my comfort, as you claim. I put it up to the teeth, and properly. I didn't see the girl.

Mencken

That girl is none the less unquestionably just the wife for you. The trouble with ninety-nine out of one hundred men is that they marry girls whom they have carefully appraised from head to toe. Their disillusion is therefore all too quick. But in a case like yours, your attention would be claimed primarily by the girl's teeth; you wouldn't begin to notice the rest of her until long after most husbands are already tired of their wives; you would thus be contented and happy for an unusually long period.

Nathan

I go with you only half a block. The happiest marriage is not that which defers disillusion, but that which admits it at the outset. Few marriages in which the man is over forty and the woman over thirty ever turn out unhappily. Age is happy; youth, unhappy. Illusion is the happiness of the heart; disillusion is the merriment of the mind. I apologize for the platitudes. I am never strikingly original until after I've had my bath.

Mencken

Behold, the night cometh when even a bath will fail. You are, by the calendar, already at the edge of forty years. As a practical mammal you are nearer sixty. On no distant day your physician will ban the shower-bath for your heart's sake, as he already bans fried scallops and marsh-mallows for the sake of your tummy. Can you drink as much as you used to? You cherish the illusion that you can, but the sphygmomanometer tells a different tale. What of that ale-party? It damn nigh killed you. Can you work as much as you could, say, in 1902? Do you fence any more? How long has it been since you jumped over a bale of hay? Nay, you deteriorate, and not only physically, but also spiritually. Nature abhors the intellect. Its aim is always to reduce all men to the level of so many Ph.D.'s. You are on your tragic way, not only toward gout and astigmatism, but also toward platitude. Well, marriage is the supreme platitude. *Verbum Sap.*

Nathan

What you propose is simply spiritual suicide. You ask me to cut my throat on the ground that I may be down with Bright's disease in 1945.

Mencken

In a sense, yes. But you forget the one great virtue of death: it is comfortable. So is marriage — if one is old enough. As for me, I am still too young. In a very real sense I don't know my own mind.

Nathan

Yet you presume to read mine. I tell you, once and for all time, that the idea of marriage is objectionable to me. The very mention of it perturbs me. I dislike your talk of it as much as I dislike your constant gabble about embolisms, staphylococci, compound fractures and nitrobenzol fumigation. Shut up.

Mencken

Again I point to Freud. To me the thought of marriage is not obnoxious, and for a very simple reason; I stand in no danger of it. No doubt there are women in the world who would marry me, at least in preference to going on the street, but I must confess humbly that their willingness seldom shows itself exigently. But that is not the main thing. The main thing is that I stand in no *need* of marriage — that I am quite as safe and comfortable now, on my estates in Maryland, as I would be with a wife, or even six wives. Thus there is no subconscious pull in me in favour of it, and so I can contemplate it without choler. Well, the very fact that you can't is proof of your inner inclination — of the hard pull of the subtle and infallible instinct that safeguards the individual. The powers and principalities of the air root for your union to some amiable and watchful miss. You are nominated for the altar by a just and omnipotent God. Your reluctance begins to verge upon blasphemy. Moreover, it is idiotic. You'd be better off if —

Nathan

Permit me, friend Strindberg, to judge of that for myself. I —

Mencken

Hollow words. Idle words. You are the worst of all possible judges of your own advantage. It would be cruel to hand you over to your own mercies. Suppose I had done it in the matter of your lumbago? You'd have been on crutches by now, and fed from a spoon. Suppose I had done it in the matter of that Belgian countess? You'd have —

Nathan

I return the ball, and with a wallop. I have saved you at least ten times, not only from bankruptcy and fatal disease, but also and especially from women. Well, I now continue my good offices. That is, I counsel you to marry and settle down. Put the whole business into my hands. I'll find the girl, see that she has enough money to support you decently, and arrange all the details. And if she is short of money, then I'll at least make sure that she has a kind heart. I am astounded that a man as vain as you are hasn't got himself lawful offspring long ago. You regard your very existence as a great favour to the Republic. When you speak of your family, it is in the tones proper for speaking of 1884 Tinta Amarella, or the Battle of Agincourt, or the bones of St. Chrysostum. I know all the chief snobs of New York, but you are one of the damndest. Well, what fetches me is this: if you are actually the superb creature that you say you are, then why don't you perpetuate yourself in the traditional manner? Can it be that you are really willing to let your race die out when you yourself are shoveled into the crematory? I should think that your patriotic feelings would revolt against the idea. You should put it away as unmanly and anti-social. Year pursues year. You are older than I am. What I propose is that you forthwith do your duty to your family, to your country and to posterity. Shoulder arms! March!

Mencken

With all due respect, I decline unqualifiedly. The Republic has yet to reward me suitably for inhabiting it. I make a sacrifice, but get no thanks. In fact, whenever I hear the matter discussed at all, the prevailing view of Americans is that I'd achieve a public boon by getting out. Such is the gratitude of an unimaginative, envious and ignoble people.

If, now, I should put my inclination and best interests upon the altar and found a family, it would be supererogation. Moreover, I doubt that my children would be appreciated any more than I am. After they had passed their nonage in my society, imbibing my prejudices, it would take artillery or a convulsion of nature to convert them into 100% Americans, or even into one-half of 1% Americans. The chances are, indeed, that they'd be sent to Atlanta Prison at birth, or, at all events, as soon as they were confirmed. This would grieve my wife, probably a respectable and right-thinking young woman.

Nathan

Don't worry. Your wife would train them, not you. They would live to be ashamed of your holiest sentiments, as they would be ashamed of your hat and overcoat. I venture to predict that if you ever have a son he will die a Methodist bishop. Your oldest daughter will be a professor of rhythmic dancing in some woman's college. The twins will run for Congress.

Mencken

You sicken me. I positively gag. Lay off, I prithee!

Nathan

Very well, but I demand tit for tat. Have done with your grisly chatter about marrying me off to get me a nurse when my knees give out, and I'll give up talking about your progeny. Is it a bargain?

Mencken

I —

(*Unearthly yells are heard in the next cell.*)

Nathan

What is that?

Mencken

The Irishman has tackled De Wolf Hopper.

Nathan

(*Leaping into his pantaloons.*)
Let us get out of here!

                    Mencken
(*Pulling his shirt over his head.*)
I am with you!

(*They exit precipitately.*)
————————————

Conversation IX: "On the Darker Races"

Scene: *The Crystal Room at the Ritz.*

Time: *During Supper.*

Mencken

The point, of course, is delicate, and I hope you forgive me for raising it. Nevertheless, I conceive it to be my duty to venture upon an animadversion.

Nathan

Speak freely, I pray you. I am surely not sensitive. But what, precisely, is the gravamen of your complaint?

Mencken

In brief, that you embarrassed me greatly in Fifth Avenue this afternoon. I grant you that the lady had a certain rich, barbaric beauty. One often notices it in the darker races, including the Hamitic. Mark Twain, as you may recall, was fond of dwelling upon it. But what I maintain is that it is unseemly for a man of your years and dignity, when walking in the principal street of the Republic with a man known to be of Southern principles, to stop stark still, crane his neck indecently, and so stand staring at a passing colored girl. The whole episode was distasteful to me.

Nathan

Nonsense. You exaggerate greatly. I by no means gaped at the lady — at all events, I gaped no more than is customary in Fifth Avenue. When a woman, whatever her race, hoofs it down such a *rue* in mid-afternoon, she plainly invites all passers-by to observe her pulchritude. If she were in a hurry, and careless of admiration, she would use Sixth Avenue, or Madison. When she turns into Fifth she hoists her pennant to the masthead, and challenges connoisseurs. Well, this fair raccoon was surely not evil to the eye, and so I gave her the small tribute of a respectful leer. She was, in fact, the most sightly baggage on view between St. Thomas' Church and Forty-second Street.

Mencken

Granted. But you overlook an important point, or, as the late Henry James had it, an implication. The aim of a woman who exhibits her person in Fifth Avenue of an afternoon is certainly not merely to give æsthetic delight to dilettanti. Her purpose is actually far more complex and daring. What she always hopes for, when she, sees some handsome buck observe her graces, is that he will be seized by an acute amorous passion, and that he will therefore track her down, get an introduction to her, woo her in the manner of James K. Hackett, and, after due formalities, marry her.

Nathan

The idea is not new. You have preached it for twenty years. But what of the fat old gals in the parade, all dolled up? They have husbands already, and presumably satisfactory ones, as their limousines show. Why should *they* break hearts?

Mencken

The fatter they are, the easier they fall. In such cases I simply exclude immediate intent. It is not in the foreground — but a husband may die at any minute. In any case, they are just as eager to be loved as a flapper. Have you ever heard of a woman who was offended by the news that some imbecile of a man had conceived an illicit passion for her? If you have any doubt in the matter, you may put it to a simple test. I suppose all experts would agree that the most beautiful moment in any marriage, to the bride, comes immediately after the rector has done his duty. She has snared her boob and has him publicly on exhibition — and there has been no time for the inevitable disillusionment. If she is not satisfied with him then, she will never be. Well, all I ask is that you go to some bride of your acquaintance at such a moment — some bride who, as the saying is, is violently in love with her victim, and intensely proud of him — go to her, take her behind one of the florist's palms, tell her flatly that you are in love with her, and propose boldly that she elope with you to Palm Beach. Add that if she refuses you will quit work, give up drink, retire to a monastery, and pine away. If she shows the slightest sign of being offended — if, in fact, she fails to glow with delight, and to give you a buss for your pains — then I shall be glad to hand you an order on my bankers for five thousand dollars cash.

Nathan

You shake me. But what has all this wisdom to do with the beautiful yaller one?

Mencken

Simply this: that the fundamental *principæ* of American *Kultur* forbid you to satisfy the expectation raised by your admiring leer. Our laws, for good or for ill, prohibit alliances between Ethiopian and Caucasian, or vice versa, and if not our laws then at least our customs, our *mores*. Thus you agitate the poor girl wantonly and to no good end. No doubt she was on Fifth Avenue in the hope that some visiting French diplomat would get mashed on her. The French not only do not forbid interracial marriages; they regard them as especially romantic. My colored ash man down in Baltimore, during his services to democracy in France, was married by public outcry to a French lady of the *bourgeoisie*. That marriage did not violate French notions of the fit and proper. The family of the bride, I daresay, would have preferred a legal ceremony, but in war-time they were willing to overlook the technicality. Moreover, the bridegroom is alive to his duty to maintain the bride according to her station in life, and sends her picture postcards every week. But suppose he proposed to bring her out to the United States, and set up housekeeping with her in Baltimore. At once the Ku Klux Klan would visit him, and tar and feather him.

Nathan

A horrible proof of the barbarism of you Southerners. As for me, though my admiration for colored beauty remains distant and academic, and it would pain me sincerely to hear that any beautiful creole was mooning about me, I must tell you flatly that I think you greatly underestimate the Afro-American character. For a Southerner, you are relatively civilized. I doubt that you have ever taken part personally in burning a concrete dinge at the stake; moreover, I hear that you treat the colored slaves on your estates very decently, and always give something to their pastor when he comes 'round with his hat. Nevertheless, you are a good Confederate at heart, and have all the prejudices that go therewith. What of the time, two or three months ago, when you smuggled in those five cases of Scharzhofberger 1908, and gave that *fête champétre* you are always talking about? Did you invite any of the local *maduro* gentry? Or did you confine the revels to Aryans?

Mencken

You talk bosh. I invented [*sic*] no Americans at all. Imagine wasting such precious stuff on an Americano! Good Moselle would gag him, even if white. If black, or brown, or puce-colored, it would kill him out of hand. When I give a soiree for the adjacent Ethiops I serve gin. It is their national drink.

Nathan

Characteristically, you now seek to becloud the issue. It is not the tastes of the darker races that we are discussing, but their social position under the Republic. If they prefer gin to the still wines, what of it? If you are ever married at all, you will have to marry a woman who drinks gin, or go out to Iowa for your bride.

Mencken

I have no plans in that direction. I admire the fair sex, but not to that degree.

Nathan

Precisely. And it is so that I admire the female Moor. I look, I raise my eyebrows, I cough respectfully, and it is over. If she gets mashed on me, it is her own fault. She is quite as well aware of the statutes against miscegenation as I am. *Caveat emptor.* Her white sisters have no laws to help them. I engaged the glance of that beauteous Senegalese this afternoon in a purely æsthetic and refined spirit. I admired her just as I might have admired "Die Meistersinger," a piece of Tiffany glass, or *faisan truffé* with *sauce chasseur.*

Mencken

I dispute your whole case. Æsthetic admiration, when it is directed toward a human female by a human male, is never free from extraneous considerations. Either there is a touch of contempt in it or a touch of reverence. It is my contention that, when you favored that colored girl with your complimentary leer this afternoon, you were far more the ex-Confederate than I am, or that I have ever been since the days of Reconstruction. In it, whether consciously or not, there was a touch of loathsome Aryan condescension. You knew very well that, had she been white, she might have complained to the police and that they would have forced you to marry her or to pay her damages. And you also knew that, being dark, she had no remedy in jurisprudence.

Nathan

No remedy? Why should she want a remedy? Does one seek a remedy against a transcendent and ineffable *plaisir*?

Mencken

Nevertheless, my point holds. All your answer says is that, in consequence of the backwardness of Negro education in the South, she was unaware of her rights, or, more precisely, of her lack of rights.

Nathan

(*He looks at his watch.*) God knows what you are talking about now. I can only repeat that I harbored no evil intention. If the poor girl cherishes my image, I can only say that I am sorry. Let her cheer up. Some go-getter of a colored bootlegger will marry her yet.

Mencken

Now you give away your whole case. Your tone indicates that, your glare, however æsthetic, was without reverence. I contend that it was thus offensive.

Nathan

But what has reverence to do with a purely æsthetic emotion? I didn't kiss her hand; I simply looked at her.

Mencken

Beauty in the human female is almost indistinguishable from reverence in the beholder. The moment a man begins to regard a woman with lofty and appreciative sentiments, that moment he begins to think of her as relatively sightly, even though she have ears like chrysanthemums and a nose like the lamented Huneker.

Nathan

Your logic, as always, has as many air-passages as a dried sponge. Pushing your reasoning to its inevitable conclusion, one must believe that because one reveres General Ulysses S. Grant more than one reveres Rodolph Valentino, the General is therefore the more elegant spectacle. You will grant readily enough, I hope, that the average married friend of ours reveres his wife more than he reveres, let us say, the late sweetie, Mile. Lantelme. But would you argue that he thinks her as beautiful?

Mencken

Most certainly. And you know it. The average married man thinks that his wife is the True Lovely One. The moment he stops thinking it, he begins to divert himself by giving booze parties, and you know how many booze parties we are ever invited to by our married friends. But again I fear that I wander. To return to the motif. The African is not beautiful to the Caucasian for the same reason that the latter is not beautiful to the African. Like likes like. It is inevitable. At least in the direction of æthetics.

Nathan

Again you fall into error. Isn't it true that a blond Caucasian nine times in ten admires a brunette Caucasian? Well, this is merely the elementary stage in the Caucasian's progress to the æsthetic goal, to his final and critically intelligent admiration of brunette beauty in its complete flower, which is to say, in the dinge. You yourself have freely admitted that the tan damsel was by all odds the best looking human being we saw on the Avenue, yet now you seek to prove that not only was she not good-looking, but that the white houris we passed (whom you have in no unmistakable terms condemned) were in comparison very lovely. You contradict yourself, Mr. Gallagher.

Mencken

Absolutely, Mr. Shean. But beauty is itself a contradiction. It goes by favor. Its springs are esoteric. Take a concrete instance. When you were younger, you considered Lillian Russell a great sight for the eyes. Think a minute; look back in your mind's eye to the Lillian Russell you then admired; regard her in terms of what you consider beautiful today. Does not she seem, in this retrospect, vastly less beautiful than you originally believed her to be?

Nathan

There you break a clay pipe! But it proves nothing. Because one's own standards of beauty change does not mean that beauty itself changes. If, tomorrow, I cease to believe that the chocolate virgin of this afternoon was beautiful, some other virtuoso, quite as *delicat* as I, will continue to regard her as beautiful. One cannot soundly criticize æsthetics in terms of one's personal, changing tastes, any more than one can say that corned beef and cabbage is not sustenance simply because one has acquired dyspepsia.

Mencken

What I object to primarily is not your philosophy, but your personal taste. How a man like you, a respectable and moral citizen of the State, the father of eight charming children, and a contributor to the Red Cross, can stoop to such æsthetic slumming, is a something that baffles me. The gal was actually very homely.

Nathan

No need for bafflement. My personal taste, as you call it, is as low as my morality is high. I admire the dark lady as I admire Mack Sennett, "Boris Godunoff," and sauerkraut. I prefer Florence Mills' singing to Sarah Bernhardt's. I hold that Bert Williams was a handsomer fellow than Lyman Abbott. I would rather watch a pretty girl dance than go to "Troilus and Cressida," "King Lear," or Chicago. And I would a damned sight rather look at our fair blackbird than at Mrs. Asquith. If this be treason, make the most of it.

Mencken

Treason, bosh! It is merely whang-doodle. You try to convince me that the autumn leaf in point was lovely simply on the ground that you *think* she was lovely. You might as well argue that democracy is sound because Brander Matthews thinks it is sound. You and Matthews, in good truth, have a lot in common. You are both essentially Puritans; all Puritans are hypocrites; and it is one of the marks of your own hypocrisy to pretend that you consider a colored gal better-looking than a white one. Yet you don't believe it for a moment. I have been to seven parties with you in the last two weeks, and you fell for a taffy blonde at every one of them. Answer that, if you can!

Nathan

The easiest thing in the world! I take profound pleasure in answering it. That answer, very simply, is this: You are right.

Mencken

But why am I right? Or, in a clearer way of putting it, why are *you* wrong?

Nathan

I may have been bibbing too much.

Mencken

No. I watched you. You didn't touch a drop after the fourteenth cocktail.

Nathan

Then ascribe it to my invariable courtesy — aye, even chivalry — toward the fair sex. If a lady (provided she be sufficiently toothsome) shows that it would please her if I made signs of admiring her, I am ever gent enough to oblige. More, I am, from long practise, able to negotiate the feat very convincingly. So convincingly, in fact, that on one occasion (the date, as I recall, was November 2, 1898) I almost convinced myself. If all the lemon méringue blondes you speak of had been pitch black, it would have been all the same to Giorgio. Social grace is social grace.

Mencken

You talk like a sophomore. You not only talk, but you lie. The truth about you is that you admired the sooty one of the Avenue not because she was a Soudanese but because she was a girl. You like gals *qua* gals, and you know it.

Nathan

Admitted. I inherited the taste from my father, and from his father before him. My great-great-grandfather, in point of tact, married six times, on the third and fourth occasions simultaneously. All these fore-bears were great connoisseurs of female beauty. My taste for the dusky, however, I did not inherit from them. That comes to me from George Washington, for whom a discerning and foreseeing papa and mamma named me.

Mencken

You were named, not for George Washington, but for George Harvey. Your estimable pa foresaw that you would grow up to be a plain damphool.

Nathan

You are up a tree, *mon cher*. You find that you have no answer to my arguments and you cover your confusion and embarrassment by calling me names. I resent the insult, though I confess there is something in it. My seconds will wait upon you in the morning.

Mencken

Let them wait. I shall leave a call for noon.

Nathan

Thus again making me edit the damned magazine while you are lolling luxuriously at your ease. What do you choose as weapons?

Mencken

I leave 'em to you.

Nathan

I name highballs.

Mencken

At twenty pesos? Never! I name lager.

Nathan

Agreed.

(*The bill is paid; they exit; they don coats, hats and sticks; they hail a taxi-cab; they run over and kill an aged negro; they arrive home; they play a duet upon the piano; they say their prayers; they retire for the night to their respective lits.*)

—————————

GLOSSARY

The Glossary is intended to provide readers with a brief description of various people, places, and things mentioned by HLM and GJN in their "Conversations." Cursory explanations of select words and phrases are offered here only as a starting point for further inquiry and should not be considered authoritative.

Abbott, Lyman (1835-1922). Recently deceased American author, theologian, and editor of *The Outlook: A Family Paper*.

Accouchement of Marie Antoinette. HLM likely refers to the series of biographical works French artist Élizabeth Vigée Le Brun painted for her patron Marie Antoinette.

Acropolis. Hilltop in Athens, Greece, and the site of the Parthenon, an iconic structure of the classical world.

Ade, George (1866-1944). Indiana-born American author, newspaper columnist and playwright. Among his many works are the humorous *Fables in Slang* (1900) and the play *The College Widow* (1904).

African. For the purposes of HLM and GJN, any black person, regardless of national origin.

Afro-American. Archaic term denoting an African American.

Allentown, Pa. Then a predominately industrial city in a largely German-American area of Pennsylvania.

Ambrose Channel. Shipping channel in the Port of New York and New Jersey.

American Credo, The (1920). A joint work by GJN and HLM, *The American Credo* contained a series of clever witticisms, many of which originally appeared in *The Smart Set*.

American Magazine. A monthly, the *American Magazine* was created by the merger of several less successful magazines of the period.

Anglo-Saxon. In this usage by GJN, the English stage.

Antoinette, Marie (1774-1792). French noblewoman, last Queen of France, executed by guillotine during the French Revolution.

Antony, Marc (83-30 BCE). Roman politician and a tragic character from Shakespeare's *Antony and Cleopatra.*

Armstrong, Paul (1868-1915). American writer, producer, and director; remembered for *Alias Jimmy Valentine* (staged 1910; filmed 1915).

Aryans. GJN teases HLM about his "kind," i.e. white people of Germanic origins, and more specifically, HLM's neighbors in Baltimore.

Ash Wednesday. Christian day of fasting and prayer marking the first day in the Lenten calendar.

Asquith, Mrs. (1864-1945). Margot Asquith, author, socialite, and wife of H. H. Asquith, recently (1908-1916) Prime Minister of the United Kingdom.

Atlanta Prison. The United States Penitentiary, Atlanta.

Atlantic Monthly. Prominent American magazine founded in 1857, then edited by Ellery Sedgwick.

Austrian Tyrol. Land of spectacular vistas in western Austria located within the Eastern Alps.

B.V.D. Men's underwear brand then made by Bradley, Voorhees, and Day.

Bach, Johann Sebastian (1685-1750). German composer of the Baroque period.

Baggage. A term used by both HLM and GJN, defined in Cary's *Slang of Venery* (1916) as "a prostitute; a whore or strumpet; a woman of loose morals. The word is also a familiar colloquialism for a pert, saucy, young woman; like wench, rogue, gypsy, it is often used endearingly."

Bahr, Hermann (1863-1934). Austrian director and playwright.

Balfour, Arthur James (1848-1930). British politician and former Prime Minister; author of the Balfour Declaration (1917) supporting a Jewish homeland in Palestine.

Baltimore, Maryland. Port city on the Atlantic coast; birthplace and life-long residence of HLM.

Baptist. Protestant denomination of the Christian church for whom baptism is a central tenet.

Barker, Lewellys F. (1867-1943). Former Professor Emeritus of Medicine at Johns Hopkins University Hospital in Baltimore, Maryland.

Barrie, James M. (1860-1937). Scottish playwright and novelist, known for *Peter Pan*.

Battle of Agincourt (1415). English military victory over the French during the Hundred Years' War.

Beaux Arts. The Café des Beaux Arts at the Beaux Arts Hotel in Manhattan.

Beef Trust Burlesquers. Popular chorus line of the late 19th and early 20th century.

Beethoven, Ludwig van (1770-1827). German symphonic composer whose works were favorites of HLM.

Belasco, David (1853-1931). American author, producer, director, and highly successful theater impresario.

Bendel's. Henri Bendel of New York; a fashionable women's clothing and accessories store.

Bernhardt, Sarah (1844-1923). Iconic French stage and film actress.

Bickel, George (1863-1941). American stage and film actor.

Bierbass. A deep, bass voice.

Biltmore Hotel. The Biltmore (1913) was a fine hotel near Grand Central Terminal in Midtown Manhattan.

Binet-Simon. The Binet-Simon test, the first IQ (intelligence quotient) test was created by Albert Binet and Théodore Simon.

Bismarck, Otto von (1815-1898). German statesman and diplomat, former Chancellor of the German Empire.

Blatz, Sidney. Music-show comedian (lost to history).

Blue Laws. Typically, a local or statewide law prohibiting business activities on Sundays.

Bok, Edward W. (1863-1930). Recently retired editor of the *Ladies' Home Journal*; Pulitzer Prize winning author.

Bolivar, Patsy. A "Patsy;" one who is taken advantage of by others (based on a fictional character from the vaudeville era).

Bolshevist. A Bolshevik; a supporter of Bolshevism, a Marxist ideology advocating the overthrow of the capitalist state and the "dictatorship of the proletariat."

Boob, boobery (*booboisie*). From *bourgeoisie*, a favorite expression of HLM identifying foolish and uncultured members of American society.

Borglum, Gutzon (1867-1941). American sculptor, then involved with the Stone Mountain project in Georgia and later with Mount Rushmore in South Dakota.

Boris Godunoff. The opera by Russian composer Modest Mussorsky (1839-1881) based on the dramatic work of Aleksandr Pushkin (1799-1837) and depicting the life of Russian Tsar Boris Gudonov (1558-1605).

Brahms, Johannes (1833-1897). 19th century German composer and pianist.

Brass Check (1919). An exposé of journalism written by Upton Sinclair.

Brieux, Eugène (1858-1932). French dramatist often focusing on social inequities of the era.

Bright's. Kidney disease associated with alcohol consumption, named for English physician Richard Bright (1789-1858).

Brisbane, Arthur (1864-1936). American author and newspaper editor.

Broadway. Manhattan thoroughfare running north-south; synonymous with the New York theater district.

Brummel, Beau (1778-1840). An English "dandy," known for his taste in fashion.

Bryan, William Jennings (1860-1925). Democratic Party presidential candidate (1896, 1900, 1908) and Secretary of State under President Woodrow Wilson.

Bülow, Fürst von (1849-1929). German politician and former Chancellor, 1900-1909.

Cabell, James Branch (1879-1958). Virginia-born author of distinctive fantasy fiction whose works, including the controversial novel *Jurgen*, were often reviewed by HLM in *The Smart Set*.

Camembert. Soft French cheese made of cow's milk.

Campbell's Funeral Church. The Frank E. Campbell Funeral Chapel at Madison Avenue and 81st Street in Manhattan; known then and now for many "celebrity" funerals.

Caucasian. For the purposes of HLM and GJN in (IX), any white person.

Caveat emptor. Latin for "buyer beware."

Cellini, Benvenuto (1500-1571). Italian artist and author, remembered for his autobiography.

Century Theater. The Century Theatre, formerly at 62nd Street and Central Park West in New York.

Chambers, Robert W. (1865-1933). Prolific American author whose novels and stories were frequently adapted to silent film.

Chambertin. French red wine.

Champs Elysées. Magnificent avenue in Paris.

Chaplin, Charlie (1889-1977). English silent film star and international celebrity.

Château Thierry. French town on the Marne and the site of a military battle between U.S. and German troops during World War I.

Chautauqua. A word from the Iroquois describing a sort of social gathering then popular in rural America, originating with the Chautauqua Lake (New York) Sunday School Assembly.

Chinatown Trunk Mystery (1909). GJN refers in (VIII) to an unsolved New York murder case in which the body of young Elsie Sigel was discovered in a trunk in the apartment of her alleged lover, a Chinese man named William Leon Ling.

Christendom. The Christian world, a frequent reference of HLM, and of Frank Harris, an author and editor HLM admired.

Christian Science. The Church of Christ, Scientist, then an increasingly popular American religious movement founded by Mary Baker Eddy.

Collier, Peter Fenelon (1849-1909). American publisher and founder of *Collier's*, a weekly magazine, later edited by his son Robert J. Collier (1876-1918).

Columbia University. Ivy League school and New York's oldest university.

Comfort. Then a popular mail-order periodical.

Common Clay. The play by Cleves Kinkead, produced by A. H. (Al) Wood (below), opened at Theatre Republic on West 42nd Street in New York in August 1915. GJN was critical in his column appearing in *The Smart Set.*

Coney Island. Renowned amusement park and resort in Brooklyn, New York.

Confederate. Member or supporter of the former Confederate States of America (1861-1865).

Confucius. GJN addresses HLM as the ancient Chinese philosopher.

Congressional Record. The official journal of the United States Congress.

Congressmen. Usually unnamed but nevertheless frequent targets of HLM.

Coon. HLM and GJN both use this racial slur (among many) in Conversation IX, arguably for effect. The term has its origins in the racial stereotypes of 19th century minstrel shows, blackface performances, and "coon songs."

Corot, Jean-Baptiste-Camille (1796-1875). Prolific French artist, primarily known as a landscape and portrait painter.

Crane, Dr. Frank (1861-1928). Presbyterian minister, author, and speaker, known for his *Four Minute Essays*.

Crane, William H. (1845-1928). American stage and film actor.

Crillon. The Restaurant Crillon at Park Avenue and East 48th Street in Manhattan.

Crowninshield, Frank (1872-1947). American critic and journalist; long-time editor of *Vanity Fair*.

Crystal Room. Fine dining establishment at the Ritz-Carleton Hotel, formerly at 46th Street and Madison Avenue in Manhattan.

Curb-broker. A stockbroker of the period who literally operated out-of-doors and on the sidewalks. Curb-brokers were well-known on Broad Street in Manhattan and in financial districts in other major cities. The New York Curb Market Association (1911) is considered a precursor to the American Stock Exchange.

Curiosity. The play by H. Austin Adams ran from December 1919 through January 1920 at the Greenwich Village Theatre.

Cuspidor. Another name for a spittoon, where men would spit their tobacco juices. Common in public places, often situated on the floor, and often decorated or designed to match their surroundings.

D'Annunzio, Gabriel (1863-1938). Italian literary and nationalist political figure.

D'Indy, Vincent (1851-1931). French composer who studied under German composer César Franck.

Damphool. A damn fool.

Darker Races. It is perhaps not coincidental that Conversation IX: "On the Darker Races," shared its subtitle with an influential publication of the era, *The Crisis: Record of the Darker Races*, then edited by W. E. B. Du Bois and published by the National Association for the Advancement of Colored People (NAACP).

De Pauw University. Private university in Indiana, the state from which GJN hailed.

Debs, Eugene V. (1855-1926). American politician and frequent Socialist Party candidate for the presidency of the United States, Debs campaigned during 1920 from the Atlanta Federal Penitentiary where he was then imprisoned under the Sedition Act.

Del Pezzo's. The Del Pezzo Restaurant at West 34th Street in Manhattan.

Delmonico's. The epitome of fine dining in Manhattan, then located at Fifth Avenue and 44th Street.

Die Meistersinger. In full, *Die Meistersinger von Nürnberg*, the opera by German composer Richard Wagner (1813-1883).

Dinkelspiel, Otta. Burlesque comedian (lost to history).

Dixon, Tom (1864-1946). Thomas Dixon, Jr., American novelist and playwright, author of the book *The Clansman* (first staged in 1905; filmed in 1915 by D. W. Griffith as *The Birth of a Nation*). HLM's comment about "Tom Dixon's anti-Bolshevik play" refers to *The Red Dawn*, based on Dixon's 1909 novel, *Comrades: A Story of Social Adventure in California*. The play opened in August 1919 at the 39th Street Theatre and ran for five nights. Writing in *The Theatre, The Drama, The Girls* (1921), GJN called the play "an effort on the part of that gentleman of God to inform his people on the grave dangers of socialism." Dixon and his works are remembered as virulently racist.

Dreiser, Theodore (1871-1945). Indiana-born American novelist, often championed by HLM and a long-time Mencken correspondent.

Dressler, Marie (1868-1934). Then-popular Canadian-born actor of stage and screen.

Eleanor. HLM perhaps refers to the playwright Eleanor Gates (1874-1951), author of *The Poor Little Rich Girl* (staged 1912; filmed 1917).

Elks. In full, the Benevolent and Protective Order of Elks, a fraternal organization founded in 1868 and by its Constitution originally open exclusively to white, male Christian membership.

Episcopal. In America, the Protestant denomination resulting from the Revolutionary era separation from the (Anglican) Church of England.

Ethiopian. People of Ethiopia, the African country and ancient civilization dating back millennia. Used by HLM (Ethiopian, Ethiops) in Conversation IX as a collective term for black people, regardless of their national heritage.

Evening Post. Popular American magazine; in full, the *Saturday Evening Post*.

Fables in Slang (1900). Book by author George Ade containing material from his humorous newspaper columns.

Farley, Mr. One suspects that Mr. Farley is a bootlegger, real or imagined.

Fifth Avenue. The most desirable shopping district in Manhattan.

Follies. A woman performing in the *Ziegfeld Follies*, a popular theatrical revue.

Fort Wayne, Ind. The city of GJN's birth; named for Revolutionary War hero Anthony Wayne. Nathan's family moved from Fort Wayne to Cleveland, Ohio when he was about six years old.

Frankfurter. Tradition German pork and beef sausage.

Freud, Sigmund (1856-1939). Pioneering Austrian medical doctor and founder of psychoanalysis.

Gallagher, Mr. Half of the popular comedy duo consisting of Ed Gallagher (1873-1929) and Al Shean (1868-1949), a.k.a. Gallagher and Shean.

Garden, Mary (1874-1967). Scottish opera star.

Gettysburg Address. Iconic speech delivered by American President Abraham Lincoln after the decisive Civil War battle at Gettysburg, Pennsylvania in 1863.

Giorgio. GJN refers to himself in the third person.

Gibbons, Herbert Adams (1880-1934). American journalist and foreign correspondent.

Giroflé-Giroflá. An operetta by French composer Charles Lecocq (1832-1918).

Gladstone, William Ewart (1809-1898). English politician and late 19th century Prime Minister of the United Kingdom.

Godey's Lady's Book. Popular 19th century American women's magazine.

Goethe, Johann Wolfgang von (1749-1832). German author and diplomat; revered as the greatest writer in the German language.

Goldberg cartoon. Referencing the popular American cartoonist Rube Goldberg (1883-1970).

Golgotha. Reference to Calvary outside Jerusalem where Jesus was crucified.

Gorki, Maxim (1868-1936). Revolutionary-era Russian-Soviet author Maxim Gorky; frequently nominated for (but never awarded) the Nobel Prize in Literature.

Grand Archons. Senior and most esteemed leaders of the fraternal organization Knights of Pythias.

Grant, Ulysses S. (1822-1885). Civil War era Commanding General of the Union Army and 18th President of the United States.

Green, Helen (1882-?). The author and journalist Helen Green van Campen, noted for her collection *At the Actor's Boarding House and Other Stories*.

Greenwich Village. Bohemian heart of lower Manhattan in the 1920s.

Griffith, D. W. (1875-1948). American director of motion pictures (including *The Birth of a Nation*) and a founder of United Artists studios.

Gustavus. GJN's given name Latinized.

Hackett, James K. (1869-1926). Canadian-born American stage and film actor.

Hamburg steak. The hamburger, made of ground beef, was popularized by German immigrants to the United States.

Hamitic. Euro-colonial racial identifier once used to represent various people of African origins.

Harris, Corra (1869-1935). American author, journalist, and war correspondent.

Harris, Frank (1855-1931). Irish American author and magazine editor of the period, known for his sexually explicit memoirs.

Harvey, George (1864-1928). George Brinton McClellan Harvey, American author, diplomat, and magazine editor.

Hawtrey, Charles (1858-1923). English actor and director.

Heart of Darkness (1899). The novel by Joseph Conrad.

Helmer, Nora. Nora Helmer, the protagonist, and her husband Torvald are characters in Henrik Ibsen's play, *A Doll's House*.

Henry. HLM refers to himself in third person.

Herr Kollege. GJN addresses HLM formally and in German as "colleague."

Hitchcock, Raymond (1865-1929). American stage and silent film actor and producer.

Hofbräuhaus. Perhaps the Hofbräuhaus at Broadway and 30th, or one of many similar establishments in Manhattan during this era.

Hopper, De Wolf (1858-1935). American actor in vaudeville and musical theater, one-time husband of popular gossip columnist Hedda Hopper, remembered for his performances of Ernest Thayer's poem "Casey at the Bat."

Hotel Continental. Then a fine hotel across from the Tuileries Garden in Paris.

Hotel Gotham. The Gotham Hotel (built in 1905) at Fifth Avenue and 55th Street in Manhattan.

Howe, E. W. (1853-1937). Indiana-born American novelist, editor, and publisher of the magazine *E. W. Howe's Monthly*, a favorite of HLM.

Hugo, Victor (1802-1885). French poet, novelist, and playwright.

Humpen. German beer mug.

Huneker, James Gibbons (1857-1921). Recently deceased author and critic admired by both HLM and GJN.

Ibáñez, Blasco (1867-1928). Spanish politician and popular novelist.

Ibsen, Henrik (1828-1906). Norwegian playwright and director.

Imagism. Literary movement in poetry then championed by Ezra Pound, who acted as an occasional European manuscript scout for *The Smart Set*.

Inauguration Ball. An Inaugural Ball is a formal celebration conducted upon the swearing-in of the President of the United States.

Infra dig. In English usage, a shortening of the Latin phrase "infra dignitatem," meaning something is below one's dignity.

Invincibilia Greco Splenderoso Superbo. In GJN's usage, perhaps a fine cigar.

Italians. People from Italy, especially Italian immigrants then coming to the United States.

Jacksonian Democracy. 19th century American political movement giving most white men over 21 years of age the right to vote.

James, Henry (1843-1916). American author and novelist who spent most of his adult life in Europe and in England.

Johns Hopkins. The Johns Hopkins University and Hospital in Baltimore, Maryland.

Jones, Evelyn. GJN (perhaps truthfully) names the woman who cleans his apartment in the Royalton.

Jones, Robert Edmond (1887-1954). American artistic designer in theater and film.

Josephus. Josephus Daniels, Secretary of the United States Navy (1913-1921) under President Woodrow Wilson.

Katzenjammer. German word for "caterwauling." Used colloquially to complain of a hangover; also a reference to the "Katzenjammer Kids," a popular comic strip of the era.

Kemp, Harry (1883-1960). American author and poet; literary tramp and occasional contributor to *The Smart Set*.

Key, Ellen (1849-1926). Swedish author, feminist, and suffragist.

Khayyam, Omar (c1048-1131). Persian author and polymathic scholar.

King Lear (c1606). The tragedy by William Shakespeare, arguably one of his greatest dramatic achievements.

Knights of Pythias. Fraternal organization founded in Washington, D.C. in 1864. For HLM, a Grand Archon would be a leader in such an organization.

Knopf, Alfred A. (1892-1984). New York publisher of books by HLM and GJN and of their next magazine endeavor the *American Mercury*.

Knox. HLM references a hat sold by the Knox Hat Company. Edward M. Knox, the Civil War era Medal of Honor recipient who operated the Knox Hat Company in the building he owned at Fifth Avenue and 40th Street in Midtown Manhattan, also where *The Smart Set* once maintained its offices.

Krausmeyer's. References to Krausmeyer's and Emil Krausmeyer are from *Krausmeyer's Alley*, a long-running though relatively undocumented burlesque show of the late 19th and early 20th centuries.

Ku Klux Klan. American white-supremacist organization founded after the Civil War; then undergoing a second genesis in the United States.

L.L.D. Doctor of Laws, an advanced academic degree.

Lake Mohonk Conference. The annual Lake Mohonk (New York) Conference on International Arbitration (1895-1916).

Lantelme, Geneviève (1883-1911). French stage actress who died under mysterious circumstances, falling from her husband Alfred Edwards' yacht.

Lawson, Thomas W. (1857-1925). American businessman; fiction and non-fiction author.

League of Nations (1920-1946). The first modern-era international organization of its kind devoted to the pursuit of peace, founded after the First World War.

Lewis, Sinclair (1885-1951). American novelist and Nobel Prize laureate.

Liedertafel. Traditional German men's choir.

Kike. An ethnic slur against Jews, especially recent Jewish immigrants to the United States.

Lima, O. County seat of Allen County, Ohio, a city just over sixty miles southeast of Fort Wayne, Indiana (birthplace of GJN). One of HLM's frequent references to small towns in America.

Lincoln, Abraham (1809-1865). 16th President of the United States and President during the American Civil War. The Lincoln Memorial in Washington, D.C. was nearing completion at the time.

Linsensuppe. Traditional German lentil soup.

Little Church Around the Corner. The Church of the Transfiguration, an Episcopal church favored by actors on East 29th Street in Manhattan.

Livery Stable Blues. Popular song (1917) by the Original Dixieland Jazz Band.

Longue Vue. The exclusive Longue Vue Club in the suburbs of Pittsburgh, Pennsylvania.

Lorimer, George Horace (1867-1937). Editor of the *Saturday Evening Post*.

Lorraine. The Lorraine Hotel at Fifth Avenue and 45th Street in Manhattan.

Louvre. Internationally recognized art museum in Paris.

Ludwig. German composer Ludwig van Beethoven.

McClure, S. S. (1857-1949). American magazine publisher and co-founder of *McClure's Magazine*.

Maccabees. HLM references the followers of Judas Maccabeas and the 2nd century BCE Maccabean Revolt.

Maeterlinck, Maurice (1862-1949). Belgian author and playwright, Nobel Prize laureate.

Main Street (1920). The novel by Sinclair Lewis, a satire on small-town life in America.

Man and Superman (1903). The play by George Bernard Shaw.

Mansfield, Richard (1857-1907). German-born, English-trained Shakespearean actor, later an American theatrical producer. Best known for his performances in Doctor Jekyll and Mr. Hyde.

Mantell, Robert (1854-1928). Scottish Shakespearean actor frequently appearing on the Broadway stage; producer in repertoire at the 44th Street Theatre (1917-1918), known for his interpretation of King Lear.

Marcosson, Isaac (1876-1961). American author and magazine editor.

Marie. HLM perhaps refers to the actor of stage and screen Marie Dressler.

Mason, John B. (1858-1919). American stage and film actor; a performer in *Common Clay* (above).

Matteawan. The Matteawan State Hospital for the Criminally Insane, established in 1892 in Matteawan, New York.

Matthews, Brander (1852-1929). Prolific American author and professor of dramatic literature at Columbia University.

Mead's Pond. Small town in New York.

Mencken, Giuseppe da. HLM makes a fictional reference to his ancestry.

Mencken, H. L. (1880-1956). Baltimore, Maryland-born American author, critic and journalist, co-editor with George Jean Nathan of *The Smart Set* and later the *American Mercury*.

Mendelssohn, Felix (1809-1847). German composer of the Romantic period.

Methodist. Member of the Methodist Church, a Protestant Christian denomination influenced by John Wesley. Methodists were often a collective target of HLM.

Michaelmas. Annual day of Christian celebration; also denotes the beginning of the academic calendar, primarily in the United Kingdom.

Midway girl. A performer in the "girl shows" of the era.

Mills, Florence (1896-1927). Washington, D.C.-born singer and dancer, a child of formerly enslaved parents, and among the few African American artists of the period to achieve popular notoriety.

Moffett, Cleveland (1863-1926). American journalist known for mystery stories. *The Conquest of America* depicts an invasion of the U.S. by Germany.

Molière (1622-1673). French actor and playwright; revered as one of the greatest French writers.

Montmartre. An area in Paris known for the arts and for its nightlife.

Moor. An archaic reference to a black person, also used to describe a Shakespearean character in *Othello*.

Moose. In full, the Royal Order of Moose, founded in 1888, and by its Constitution originally open exclusively to white, male Christian membership.

More, Paul Elmer (1864-1937). American journalist, later known for his work in the genre of Christian apologetics.

Morgan, Jim. The protagonist (a reformed drunkard) in Timothy Shay Arthur's *Ten Nights in a Bar Room*.

Moselle. A white wine, named for the Moselle River in Europe.

Mozart, Wolfgang Amadeus (1756-1791). Prolific German composer of the Classical period.

Muldoon's Health Farm. A reference to Olympia, the early 20th century health clinic and celebrity spa run by championship wrestler of the Greco-Roman style and occasional actor William Muldoon (1845-1933) on his farm in Westchester County, New York.

Mummer. The Mummers are elaborately costumed street performers whose traditions, reflected in the New Years' Day Mummers Parade in Philadelphia, date back hundreds of years.

Munsey, Frank (1854-1925). American magazine editor and publisher of *Munsey's Magazine*, later entitled *Argosy Magazine*.

Nathan, George Jean (1882-1958). Fort Wayne, Indiana-born American author and theater critic; co-editor with H. L. Mencken of *The Smart Set* and later the *American Mercury*.

Negro. An archaic racial reference meaning "black" in Portuguese and Spanish.

Nietzsche, Friedrich (1844-1900). German philosopher and the subject of an earlier work by Mencken.

New York Times. National newspaper of record.

New York. The long-time residence of GJN and location of *The Smart Set* offices.

O You Kid. A popular phrase in songs of the era; referring to attractive young women.

Odd Fellows. In full, the Independent Order of Odd Fellows, founded in Baltimore in 1819 and based on an earlier English fraternal organization.

Oh How I Love Jesus (1855). A hymn by the English priest Frederick Whitfield.

Olympic Theater. GJN refers to a later iteration of the Olympic Theater on East 14th Street in Manhattan.

Olympus. The highest mountain in Greece and, in ancient Greek mythology, the seat of the gods.

Ph.D. Doctor of Philosophy, an advanced academic degree.

Palm Beach. Palm Beach, Florida, a luxury winter residence for the well-to-do.

Paris. Paris, France.

Pas seul. GJN makes a reference from the French to dance; i.e. a "solo dance."

Pater, Walter (1839-1894). English author and critic.

Patterson, Nan (c1882-?) The New York "show girl" Nan Patterson was tried twice for the 1904 murder of Caesar Young. Never convicted, she was released from prison in 1905.

Paul. The first century Christian apostle Paul, *geb.* (born) Saul.

Pêche Melba. A popular dessert of peaches and ice cream, created by French chef Auguste Escoffier and named for Australian opera singer Nellie Melba (1861-1931).

Pennington, Ann (1893-1971). Broadway singer and dancer, then a star of the *Ziegfeld Follies*.

Philippi. A significant Greek city of the classical period known in the modern era for its ruins.

Phillips, John (1861-1949). American magazine editor and co-founder of *McClure's Magazine*.

Pierre's. Pierre's Restaurant at East 53rd Street in Manhattan, then known for its wine room.

Pinot Chardonnay. A variety of white wine.

Pittsburgh Dispatch. Then the popular newspaper in Pittsburgh, Pennsylvania.

Pittsburgh pickle. GJN's nickname of the moment for one of Mencken's cigars. Mencken's father, August Mencken, Sr., was in the cigar business.

Plaza Hotel. Luxury hotel in Midtown Manhattan, then undergoing a major expansion.

Pottstown. Pottstown, Pennsylvania, a borough just outside Philadelphia with substantial German American roots.

Presbyterian. Reformed Protestant Christian denomination which originated in Scotland. Deacons of the church were frequent targets of HLM.

Press-agent. In the rising field of Public Relations, someone who offered stories and other information to magazines and news organizations; occasionally employed (as a last resort) by HLM and GJN to acquire material for *The Smart Set*.

Public Library. New York Public Library with its prominent lion sculptures (nicknamed Patience and Fortitude) by the sculptor Edward Clark Potter.

Puritans. Broadly speaking, a historically conservative Protestant religious stance; Puritans and Puritanism were regular targets for HLM.

Quadrilles. GJN makes a reference from the French to dance; i.e. a "square dance."

Quod erat demonstrandum. Latin for "it can be shown."

Rabelaisian. Evocative of the French Renaissance humanist François Rabelais.

Reconstruction. The American post-Civil War period (1865-1877) during which slavery was fully abolished and the former Confederates states were readmitted to the Union.

Rembrandt (1606-1669). Dutch painter Rembrandt van Rijn.

Remnant. The play by Dario Niccodemi and Michael Morton ran from November 1918 through January, 1919 at the Morosco Theatre on West 45th Street.

Republic. The United States.

Rhenish Symphony (1850-1851). Robert Schumann's *Symphony No. 3,* his last symphony.

Ritz. The Ritz-Carleton Hotel, formerly at 46th Street and Madison Avenue in Manhattan.

Robey, George (1869-1954). English actor, comedian, and well-known music hall performer of the burlesque era.

Roderigo. One of the antagonists in *Othello* by William Shakespeare.

Root, Elihu (1845-1937). American politician, Secretary of State, Secretary of War, Senator of New York.

Rosenkavalier. Translated as "The Rose Bearer," a suite by German composer Richard Strauss.

Royalton. GJN lived for most of his adult life in the Royalton, then a residential hotel near Times Square.

Russell, Lillian (1861-1922). Popular American actress and singer on stage and in film.

Saint Saëns, Camille (1835-1921). French composer of the Romantic period.

Satie, Erik (1866-1925). Solitary French composer and pianist.

Saturday Evening Post. Then a weekly and one of the most widely read magazines in America.

Saukville. A small town and suburb of Milwaukee in Wisconsin.

Scandinavian. HLM refers broadly to Denmark, Norway, and Sweden.

Scharzhofberger. A fine German Riesling white wine.

Schubert, Franz (1797-1828). Short-lived yet prolific Austrian composer.

Schumann, Robert (1810-1856). 19th century German composer and critic.

Schumann-Heink, Ernestine (1861-1936). Austrian American opera singer of German Bohemian descent.

Sedgwick, Ellery (1872-1960). Then editor and owner of the *Atlantic Monthly*.

Senegalese. A person from Senegal, then still a French colony. In Conversation IX, GJN refers to the woman who is the subject of their conversation by casual or perhaps stereotypical assumption of her national origin.

Sennett, Mack (1880-1960). Canadian-born American producer, actor, and director.

Shakespeare, William (1564-1616). English actor, poet, and playwright; revered as the greatest of English authors.

Shaw, George Bernard (1856-1950). Irish playwright, critic, and Nobel Prize laureate.

Shean, Mr. Half of the popular comedy duo consisting of Ed Gallagher (1873-1929) and Al Shean (1868-1949), a.k.a. Gallagher and Shean.

Shoe-drummer. A dancer in a chorus-line of other musical revue; in this usage by HLM an undistinguished dancer among many such dancers.

Siddall, John M. (1874-1923). Then editor of the *American Magazine*.

Sinclair, Upton (1878-1968). Prolific American novelist; known as a "muckraker" and later a winner of the Pulitzer Prize.

Slater. The firm of J. & J. Slater in New York.

Slobbergobble. Although GJN and HLM clearly use this expression to accuse each other of speaking nonsense, it was rarely found in print during their era. Whether it then bore the same implications as it does in modern usage is unclear.

Smart Set, **The.** *The Smart Set,* a monthly, was published 1900-1930 and edited by HLM and GJN during the years 1914-1923.

Smith, Hoke (1855-1931). United States Senator representing the State of Georgia (1911-1920).

Smith, Tom. Thomas Robert "T. R." Smith (1880-1942), editor with the *Century Magazine* and publisher Boni & Liveright. Known for his edition of Baudelaire (1919), his *Poetica Erotica* (1921) and, perhaps more famously, for his supposedly ether-laced cocktails. HLM fondly makes him German, hence Tom Schmidt.

Socialists. Advocates of Socialism, a political philosophy akin to Communism advocating for social ownership of the economic means of production.

Sonora. A fine Mexican wood carving.

Sophocles (5th century, BCE). Classical Greek tragedian, author of *Oedipus Rex, Antigone,* etc.

Southerner. HLM identifies himself as a Southerner in rather pejorative terms and ascribes to himself certain racial prejudices associated with the post-Civil War era and Reconstruction in the southern states.

Spero che abbiate.... Speaking in Italian, GJN hopes HLM has enough money for cab fare. In response, HLM indicates that he does.

St. Bartholemew's. The Episcopal St. Bartholomew's Church at 325 Park Avenue in New York.

St. Chrysostum. Early (4th century) Christian author and ascetic.

St. Francis. The St. Francis Hotel in San Francisco, California.

St. Patrick's Cathedral. Catholic cathedral in Midtown Manhattan, designed by architect James Renwick.

St. Thomas Church. Located in Midtown Manhattan at 53rd Street and Fifth Avenue.

Star-Spangled Banner. Patriotic song (lyrics by Francis Scott Key, 1812) and the American national anthem.

Sterling, George (1869-1926). San Francisco area poet and playwright; correspondent of HLM.

Stowe, Harriet Beecher (1811-1896). American writer and abolitionist.

Strindberg, August (1849-1912). Prolific Swedish author, playwright, and novelist.

Tagore, Rabindranath (1861-1941). Indian author, philosopher, and Nobel Prize laureate.

Ten Nights in a Bar Room. The temperance novel (1854) by Timothy Shay Arthur (1809-1885), filmed (silent) in 1910.

Tewksbury. GJN perhaps refers to noted American athlete of track and field and Olympic gold medalist Walter Tewksbury.

Tiergarten. An urban park in Berlin.

Tiffany. Fine decorative art glass produced by the New York studio of Louis Comfort Tiffany (1848-1933).

Tiger! Tiger! The play by Edward Knoblock opened at the Belasco Theatre on 44th Street and ran from November 1918 through April 1919.

Timothy. The first century Christian traveler associated with Saint Paul.

Tinta Amarella. A variety of grape used to produce Port and other red wines.

Tolstoi, Leo (1828-1910). Leo Tolstoy, a Russian author of aristocratic birth; frequently nominated for (but never awarded) the Nobel Prize in Literature.

Toots. In Maitland's *Slang Dictionary* (1891), "off on toots" means "off on a drunk."

Toss the Pot. Drinking song attributed to English musician Thomas Ravenscroft (1588-1635).

Traviata. *La traviata* (The Fallen Woman), an opera (1853) by Giuseppe Verdi.

Tristan und Isolde. Romantic opera by the German composer Richard Wagner, based on a 12th century story by Gottfried von Strassburg.

Troilus and Cressida (c1602). A play by William Shakespeare, set during the Trojan War, noted as one of Shakespeare's "problem plays."

Trouville Casino. A popular gambling establishment in Normandy, France.

Twain, Mark (1835-1910). The iconic American writer and public speaker, a.k.a. Samuel Clemens.

Union Hill, N.J. Former town in Hudson County, New Jersey that merged with East Hoboken in 1925 to form Union City, New Jersey.

Union League Club. Founded in New York in 1863 in opposition to Confederate sympathizers.

Up in Mabel's Room. The play by Wilson Collison and Otto Hauerbach, produced by A. H. (Al) Woods (below), opened at the Eltinge 42nd Street Theatre in January 1919. GJN, writing in his *Comedians All* (1919), called it "a tenth-rate play."

Valentino, Rodolph (1895-1926). Rudolph Valentino, the Italian actor and silent film star.

Verbum Sap. Latin for "enough said."

Volstead Act (1919). The legislation establishing Prohibition, through the 18th Amendment to the Constitution.

Wanze. German for bug.

Washington, George (1732-1799). Leader of the American forces during the American Revolution and the first President of the United States.

Whang-doodle. An imaginary being of undefined characteristics.

Whitefield, Ann. Protagonist in the play *Man and Superman* by George Bernard Shaw.

Whytal, Russ (1860-1930). American actor and playwright.

Williams, Burt (1874-1922). Bahamian-born Vaudeville entertainer, actor, comedian and recording artist; among the few African American artists of the period to achieve popular notoriety.

Williams, John (1903-1983). Perhaps a reference to the youthful English stage and film actor.

Wilson, Woodrow (1856-1924). The 28th President of the United States (1913-1921) and a frequent target of HLM.

Wood, General (1860-1927). Major General Leonard Wood, Medal of Honor recipient and commander of the Rough Riders (with Theodore Roosevelt) during the Spanish-American War.

Woods, Al (1870-1951). Hungarian-born Broadway producer who brought well over a hundred theatrical productions to the stage.

Y.M.C.A. Acronym for Young Men's Christian Association, a world-wide youth organization founded in London in 1844.

Youngstown, Ohio. Primarily an industrial city in the 1920s.

Ziegfeld, Florenz (1867-1932). American theatrical impresario, remembered for the *Ziegfeld Follies* musical and dance revue.

Ziggy. Florenz Ziegfeld and his *Ziegfeld Follies*.

SOURCES

Ink-on-paper issues of *The Smart Set* are scarce in the antiquarian marketplace, but copies of the magazine are still available in this format in some academic and institutional libraries. The transcriptions herein were made from issues of the magazine appearing on microfilm and in publicly accessible online databases.

The microfilm edition of *The Smart Set* held by the Library of Congress is complete; however, the reproduction quality suffers from defects typical of the mass-microfilm era, including blurred or missing text and the occasional misplacement or omission of the magazine's Table of Contents.

The Hathi Trust online database reproduces editions of *The Smart Set* from the holdings of the University of California, the University of Michigan, Harvard University, and other academic institutions. Though incomplete in terms of coverage, issues of *The Smart Set* appearing in *The Hathi Trust* online database are searchable.

The *Internet Archive* contains what at first appears to be a complete run of the magazine, but several issues in this online database are of the English edition, which is distinguished from the American edition by the inclusion or exclusion of various articles by different writers. Issues of *The Smart Set* appearing in the *Internet Archive* are also searchable.

From the online reader's perspective, the *Modernist Journals Project* provides the best visual experience for accessing *The Smart Set*. Issues of the magazine were provided for use by the *Modernist Journals Project* by Johns Hopkins University in Baltimore, Maryland. Though its coverage is also incomplete, the reproduction quality realized by the *Modernist*

Journals Project reveals the covers of *The Smart Set* magazine in vivid colors and provides the best clarity for page-by-page viewing of the text. The *Modernist Journalist Project* is also searchable.

The Smart Set "Conversations"

Conversation I: "On Theater-Going" originally appeared in *The Smart Set*: Volume 62, Number 4 (August 1920), pp. 51-54, as the introductory portion of a recurring column entitled "Répétition Générale," signed under the joint byline of George Jean Nathan and H. L. Mencken.

Conversation II: "On Anatomy and Physiology" originally appeared in *The Smart Set*: Volume 63, Number 4 (December 1920), pp. 93-98, signed under the byline "Set Down by Major Owen Hatteras."

Conversation III: "On Women" originally appeared in *The Smart Set*: Volume 64, Number 1 (January 1921), pp. 71-76, signed under the byline "Set Down by Major Owen Hatteras."

Conversation IV: "On Politics" originally appeared in *The Smart Set*: Volume 64, Number 2 (February 1921), pp. 93-98, signed under the byline "Set Down by Major Owen Hatteras."

Conversation V: "On Literature" originally appeared in *The Smart Set*: Volume 64, Number 4 (April 1921), pp. 89-94, signed under the byline "Set Down by Major Owen Hatteras."

Conversation VI: "On Dress" originally appeared in *The Smart Set*: Volume 65, Number 1 (May 1921), pp. 97-102, signed under the byline "Set Down by Major Owen Hatteras."

Conversation VII: "On Editing a Magazine" originally appeared in *The Smart Set*: Volume 65, Number 2 (June 1921), pp. 99-106, signed under the byline "Set Down by Major Owen Hatteras."

Conversation VIII: "On Marriage" originally appeared in *The Smart Set*: Volume 65, Number 3 (July 1921), pp. 91-96, signed under the byline "Set Down by Major Owen Hatteras."

Conversation IX: "On the Darker Races" originally appeared in *The Smart Set*: Volume 70, Number 3 (March 1923), pp. 93-98, signed under the byline "Set Down by Major Owen Hatteras, D.S.O."

Articles, Books and Pamphlets (Cited/Consulted)

Adler, Betty, compiler, with the Assistance of Jane Wilhelm. *H. L. M.: The Mencken Bibliography*. Baltimore: The Johns Hopkins Press, 1961.

Angoff, Charles. *H. L. Mencken: A Portrait from Memory*. New York: Thomas Yoseloff, 1956.

Angoff, Charles. *The World of George Jean Nathan*. New York: Alfred A. Knopf, 1952.

Bode, Carl. *Mencken*. Carbondale: Southern Illinois University Press, 1969.

Bode, Carl, editor. *The New Mencken Letters*. New York: The Dial Press, 1977.

Bode, Carl. *The Young Mencken*. New York: The Dial Press, 1973.

Caldwell, Mark. *A Short History of Rudeness: Manners, Morals, and Misbehavior in Modern America*. New York: St. Martin's Press, 2000.

Cary, Henry Nathaniel. *The Slang of Venery and its Analogues*. Chicago: [Privately Printed], 1916.

Connolly, Thomas F. *George Jean Nathan and the Making of Modern American Drama Criticism*. Madison: Fairleigh Dickinson University Press, 2000.

Curtiss, Thomas Quinn. *The Smart Set: George Jean Nathan and H. L. Mencken*. New York: Applause, 1998.

Dolmetsch, Carl R. *The Smart Set: A History and Anthology*. New York: The Dial Press, 1966.

Fitzpatrick, Vincent. *"The Smart Set."* In *American Literary Magazines: The Twentieth Century*, edited by Edward E. Chielens, pp. 333-341. Westport: Greenwood Press, 1992.

Fitzpatrick, Vincent. *H. L. Mencken.* New York: Continuum, 1989.

Forgue, Guy J., editor. *The Letters of H. L. Mencken.* New York: Alfred A. Knopf, 1961.

Frey, Carroll. *A Bibliography of the Writings of H. L. Mencken.* Philadelphia: The Centaur Bookshop, 1924.

Goldberg, Isaac. *The Man Mencken: A Biographical and Critical Survey.* New York: Simon and Schuster, 1925.

Goldberg, Isaac. *The Theatre of George Jean Nathan.* New York: Simon and Schuster, 1926.

Harrison, S. L. *a.k.a. H. L. Mencken: Selected Pseudonymous Writings of H. L. Mencken.* [n.p.]: Wolf Den Books, 2005.

Hatteras, Owen (H. L. Mencken and George Jean Nathan). *Pistols for Two.* New York: Alfred A. Knopf, 1917.

Hobson, Fred. *Mencken: A Life.* New York: Random House, 1994.

Joshi, S. T. *H. L. Mencken: An Annotated Bibliography.* Lanham: The Scarecrow Press, 2009.

Joshi, S. T., editor. *From Baltimore to Bohemia: The Letters of H. L. Mencken and George Sterling.* Madison and Teaneck: Fairleigh Dickinson University Press, 2001.

Kemler, Edgar. *The Irreverent Mr. Mencken.* Boston: Little, Brown and Company, 1950.

Lazarus, A. L. *A George Jean Nathan Reader.* Rutherford: Fairleigh Dickinson University Press, 1990.

Loughery, John. *Alias S. S. Van Dine.* New York: Charles Scribner's Sons, 1992.

Maitland, James. *The American Slang Dictionary.* Chicago: R. J. Kittredge & Co., 1891.

Manchester, William. *Disturber of the Peace: The Life of H. L. Mencken.* Second edition. Amherst: University of Massachusetts Press, 1986.

Mayfield, Sara. *The Constant Circle: H. L. Mencken and His Friends.* New York: Delacorte Press, 1968.

Mencken, H. L. *A Book of Burlesques.* New York: Alfred A. Knopf, 1921.

Mencken, H. L. *A Little Book in C Major.* New York: John Lane Company, 1916.

Mencken, H. L. *A Personal Word.* [Baltimore or New York: Issued for Readers of *The Smart Set*], 1922.

Mencken, H. L. *Damn! A Book of Calumny.* New York: Philip Goodman, 1918.

Mencken, H. L. *In Defense of Women.* New York: Alfred A. Knopf, 1918.

Mencken, H. L. *My Life as Author and Editor.* Edited and with an Introduction by Jonathan Yardley. New York: Alfred A. Knopf, 1993.

Mencken, H. L. *H. L. Mencken. Prejudices: The Complete Series.* Edited by Marion Elizabeth Rodgers. Two volumes. New York: Library of America, 2010.

Mencken, H. L. *The Diary of H. L. Mencken.* Edited by Charles A. Fecher. New York: Alfred A. Knopf, 1989.

Mencken, H. L. and George Jean Nathan. *Heliogabalus.* New York: Alfred A. Knopf, 1920.

Mott, Frank Luther. *A History of American Magazines.* "*The Smart Set.*" Vol. 5, pp. 246-272. Cambridge: Harvard University Press, 1968.

Nathan, George Jean. *A Book Without a Title.* New York: Alfred A. Knopf, 1918.

Nathan, George Jean. *Another Book on the Theatre.* New York: B. W. Huebsch, 1915.

Nathan, George Jean. *Bottoms Up: An Application of the Slapstick to Satire*. New York: Philip Goodman Company, 1917.

Nathan, George Jean. *Comedians All*. New York: Alfred A. Knopf, 1919.

Nathan, George Jean. *The Intimate Notebooks of George Jean Nathan*. New York: Alfred A. Knopf, 1932.

Nathan, George Jean. *Mr. George Jean Nathan Presents*. New York: Alfred A. Knopf, 1917.

Nathan, George Jean. *The Popular Theatre*. New York: Alfred A. Knopf, 1918.

Nathan, George Jean and H. L. Mencken. *The American Credo: A Contribution Toward the Interpretation of the National Mind*. New York: Alfred A. Knopf, 1920.

Nolte, William H. *H. L. Mencken: Literary Critic*. Middletown: Wesleyan University Press, 1966.

Rascoe, Burton and Groff Conklin, editors. *The Smart Set Anthology*. New York: Reynal & Hitchcock, 1934.

Riggio, Thomas P., editor. *Dreiser-Mencken Letters: The Correspondence of Theodore Dreiser & H. L. Mencken, 1907-1945*. Two volumes. Philadelphia: University of Pennsylvania Press, 1986.

Rodgers, Marion Elisabeth. *H. L. Mencken and the Alt-Right*. In *Menckeniana*, Spring, 2016, pp. 13-22.

Rodgers, Marion Elizabeth. *Mencken: The American Iconoclast*. New York: Oxford University Press, 2005.

Sanders, Jack, ed. *Do You Remember?* Baltimore: Maryland Historical Society, 1996.

Schrader, Richard J. *H. L. Mencken: A Descriptive Bibliography*. Pittsburgh: University of Pittsburgh Press, 1998.

Scruggs, Charles. *The Sage in Harlem: H. L. Mencken and the Black Writers of the 1920s*. Baltimore: The Johns Hopkins University Press, 1984.

Teachout, Terry. *The Skeptic: A Life of H. L. Mencken*. New York: HarperCollins Publishers, 2002.

Williams, William H. A. *H. L. Mencken Revisited*. New York: Twayne Publishers, 1998.

Databases (Consulted)

Hathi Trust Digital Library (www.hathitrust.org)
Internet Archive (www.archive.org)
Internet Broadway Database (www.ibdb.com)
Internet Movie Database (www.imdb.com)
JSTOR (www.jstor.org)
Modernist Journals Project (www.modjourn.org)
Newspapers (www.newspapers.com)

Magazines and Newspapers (Cited/Consulted)

The Brooklyn *Daily Eagle*
The Buffalo *Evening News*
The *Forward*
Menckeniana
The *New York Times*
The Smart Set

NOTES

[1] Quoted in Dolmetsch, p. 6.

[2] Caldwell, p. 19.

[3] Mott, p. 249.

[4] Dolmetsch, pp. 24-25; Douglas, "The *Smart Set*," p. 72; Fitzpatrick, "The *Smart Set*," p. 334.

[5] Bode, *Mencken*, p. 20; Fitzpatrick, *Mencken*, pp. 3-4; Goldberg, *Mencken*, pp. 93-94.

[6] Curtiss, pp. 4-7; Lazarus, p. 15-16.

[7] Manchester, p. 39.

[8] Mayfield, p. 13.

[9] Mencken, *Life*, p. 304.

[10] Bode, *The Young Mencken*, p. 535.

[11] Dolmetsch, p. 54.

[12] Custiss, pp. 108-109; Dolmetsch, pp. 44-45; Goldberg, *Mencken*, p. 187-188; Mencken, *A Personal Word*, p. 2.

[13] Mencken, *Life*, p. 43.

[14] Dolmetsch, p. 47; Douglas, "The Smart Set," p. 77.

[15] Mencken, *A Personal Word*, pp. 2-3.

[16] Mencken, *Life*, pp. 50-51.

[17] Dolmetsch, pp. 47-48.

[18] Manchester, p. 65.

[19] Mencken, *Life*, p. 58.

[20] Nathan and Mencken, *The American Credo*, pp. 108, 113, 124, 146, 172, 183.

[21] Frey, p. 5; Mencken, *Life*, p. 323.

[22] Frey, pp. 5-6.

[23] Hatteras (Mencken and Nathan), *Pistols for Two*, p. 5.

[24] Hatteras (Mencken and Nathan), *Pistols for Two*, p. 21.

[25] Frey, p. 42.

[26] The *New York Times* (1923-); February 11th, 1951, via Pro-Quest Historical Newspapers, p. 185.

[27] Mencken, *Life*, p. 198.

[28] Douglas, "The *Smart Set*," p. 88.

[29] The Brooklyn *Daily Eagle*, April 16th, 1921, p. 11.

[30] Cited in Buffalo *Evening News*, January 6th, 1921, p. 8.

[31] Cited in the San Francisco *Chronicle*, April 10th, 1921, p. 2; Curtiss, pp. 132-133; Douglas, "The *Smart Set*," pp. 85-86.

[32] Dolmetsch, p. 36.

[33] Harrison, (note), p. 160.

[34] Connolly, pp. 23-33; See also Benjamin Ivry, "We Should Talk About the Jewish Backstory of 'All About Eve,'" in The *Forward*, July 15th, 2020.

[35] Rodgers, *Alt-Right*, pp. 13-22.

[36] Goldberg, *Mencken*, pp. 189-190.

[37] Joshi, *From Baltimore to Bohemia*, p. p. 117, p. 131.

www.ingramcontent.com/pod-product-compliance
Lightning Source LLC
Chambersburg PA
CBHW060525130626
46553CB00002B/648